BUILDING THE BRITISH

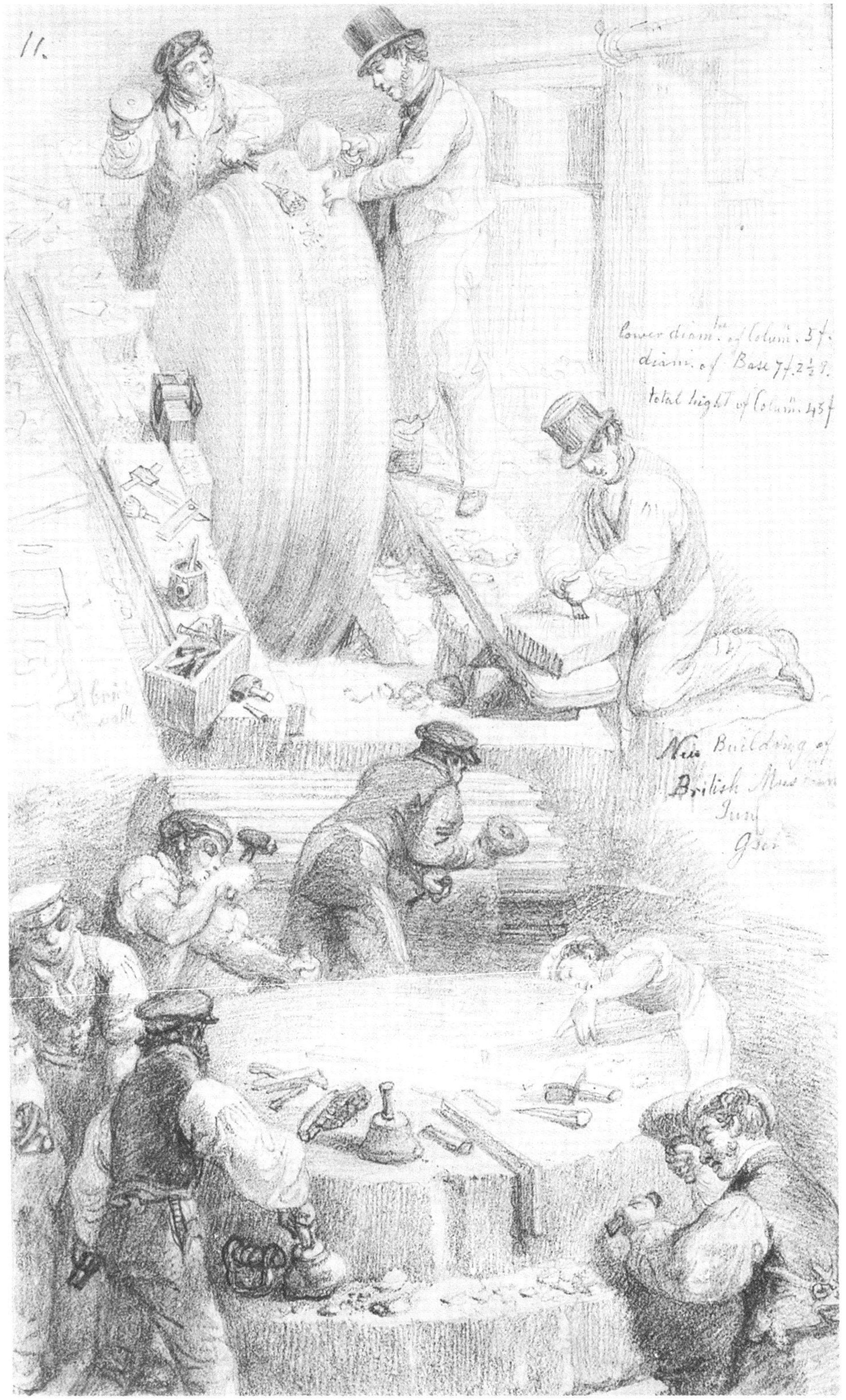
11.
lower diam.te of Colum. 5 f.
diam. of Base 7 f. 2½ I.
total hight of Colum. 45 f
New Building of
British Mus
Jun

BUILDING THE
BRITISH MUSEUM

Marjorie Caygill and Christopher Date

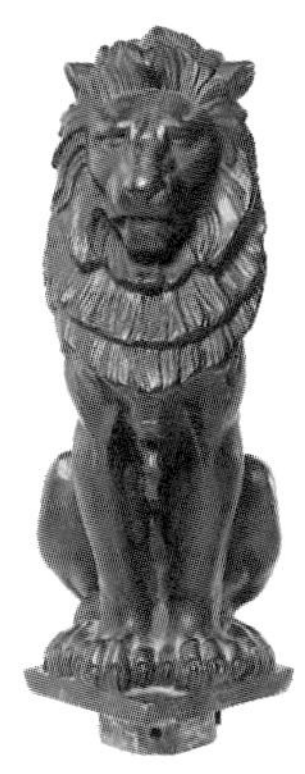

Published for The Trustees of

The British Museum by

BRITISH MUSEUM PRESS

Published by British Museum Press
A division of The British Museum Company Ltd
46 Bloomsbury Street, London WC1B 3QQ

British Library Cataloguing in Publication Data
A catalogue record for this book is available from
the British Library

ISBN 0-7141-2164-9

Designed by Martin Richards

Printed in Great Britain by
Cambridge University Press

Frontispiece: *An 1845 drawing by George Scharf showing stonemasons carving Portland stone columns for the colonnade. Scharf's attention to detail has faithfully captured the stages of this exacting work and the variety of tools required.*

Title page: *One of the twenty-five cast iron lions designed by Alfred Stevens for the southern boundary railings of 1852-96.*

PREFACE

The British Museum – the 'old curiosity shop in Bloomsbury' – has a long and tangled architectural history. At a time when interest in the building of the British Museum has been reawakened by the forthcoming completion of the Great Court in 2000 and the Museum's 250th anniversary in 2003, this book is an attempt to bring today's building alive by setting out how the pieces of an oversized jigsaw puzzle fit together, with glimpses of the individuals who (deliberately or inadvertently) made the Museum what it is today. It is intended to complement J. Mordaunt Crook's magisterial and entertaining *The British Museum: a case-study in architectural politics* (1972), which sets the building of the Museum in a wider context. We have not attempted to theorize about the architectural style of the building – this has been done by others – but rather to try to pass on some of the fascination that the building exerts and to highlight traces of the past of which visitors might otherwise be unaware.

An attempt has been made to set out definitively the dates of the various building projects. This is often difficult since, in many instances, start and completion dates were so obvious to those concerned that no one bothered to write them down, and eventually everyone forgot. A note of later alterations which brings this account of the building up to date is given in italics. In this connection, it should be noted that by the end of 1998 all library areas (printed books, manuscripts, maps, music) had been taken over for development by the Museum on the departure of the British Library to St Pancras.

A Museum habit which may bemuse visitors is that of referring to parts of the building according to the points of the compass. The building actually lies on a NE - SW plane but, for the purposes of this book and navigation on a visit, it becomes intelligible if the visitor remembers that south equals the Great Russell Street entrance and north is Montague Place. Of the floors perhaps the less said the better to avoid confusion. There are six levels including mezzanines. The principal floors are the Basements, confusingly on ground level (which contain some exhibition galleries but are largely used for storage and other purposes), the Ground Floor (the entrance level, which has the main sculpture galleries and the King's Library), and the Upper Floor (where smaller antiquities tend to be displayed).

ACKNOWLEDGEMENTS

We should like to thank our editor, Teresa Francis, who has attempted to reduce the manuscript to manageable proportions; Emma Way and Frances Carey for their support for the project; Simon Tutty and Dudley Hubbard for their assistance with photographs, and Tony Spence for his accounts of the excavations on the Museum site. The extracts from Sir Frederic Madden's diaries are quoted by permission of the Bodleian Library, University of Oxford.

Marjorie Caygill
Christopher Date

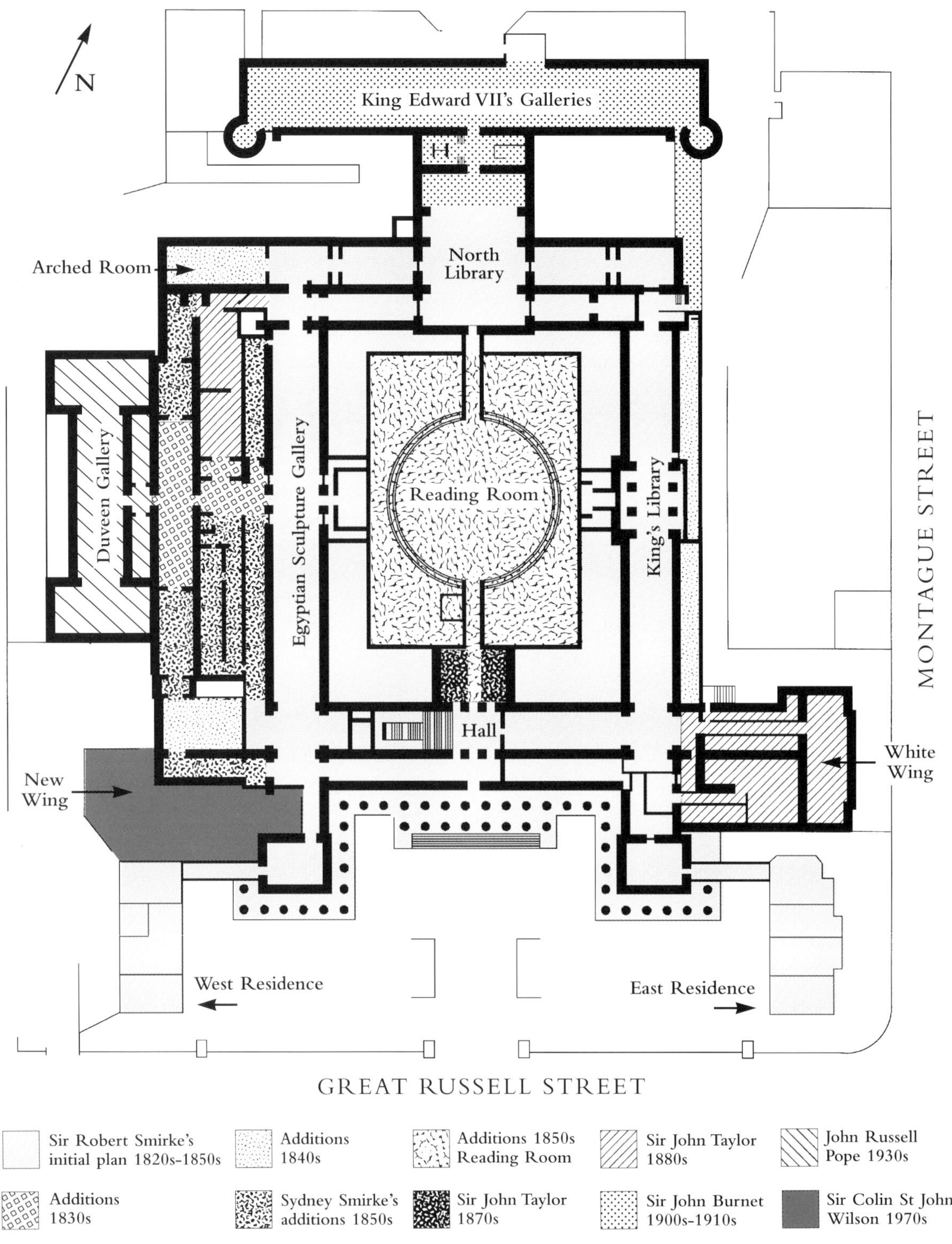

Plan of the Ground Floor showing the phases of development of the British Museum building. This is a rough guide only, since some areas have been altered on more than one occasion.

BUILDING THE BRITISH MUSEUM

> . . . although the building is not yet finished, scarcely a room remains as it was originally constructed, great alterations have been found necessary in almost all; the Building is surrounded by inconvenient and unsightly excrescences, and it may be asserted with truth, that Europe cannot show any Building so ill adapted for its intended purpose, as the British Museum.

So wrote the Keeper of Antiquities Edward Hawkins in 1851. Hawkins, who had joined the Museum in 1825, was somewhat prejudiced against novelty and was more concerned with antiquities than architecture, but he did have a point. Unravelling the history of a building which Mordaunt Crook, the architectural historian of the British Museum, described as a 'museologist's nightmare' is not easy. It does have a certain coherence but, as a nineteenth-century historian pointed out, 'At a critical time when the character of the new buildings had practically to be decided, parsimoniousness led, not only to construction piecemeal, but to the piecemeal preparation of the designs themselves . . ..'

There are drainpipes buried in the western sculpture galleries and a hidden Victorian mosaic floor still under the Architecture Room. There are unfinished bits, and bits best left unfinished. The great colonnaded south front, which for many people conjures up the very idea of a museum, was described by a Victorian commentator, not without justification, as 'a false face (though a fair one) put on a noble carcase'. On close inspection of the ends of King Edward VII's Galleries it is apparent that something is missing – namely two more wings, for it was planned as the northern section of a grandiose project to demolish the houses surrounding the Museum and replace them with splendid galleries. Numerous expediencies were introduced between the wars when the Trustees, desperate for library space, had an attack of mezzanine-building in the North Wing and produced a labyrinth which only the initiated can navigate with ease. Traces still remain of the Luftwaffe's demolition of the south-west quadrant bookstack of the library in 1941 and with it the roofs of the upper western galleries and the central saloon at the top of the main staircase. There has never been a moment in time when the 'British Museum building' existed. Instead, it has evolved.

But for all this, with old age has come respectability and a building which inspires affection. The main Museum is now a Grade I listed building – the highest conservation category – and the later King Edward VII Galleries are Grade II. The building bears the traces of nine architects: Robert Hooke (1635-1703), 'Puget' (*fl.* 1678, so far not positively identified), George Saunders (*c.*1762-1839), Sir Robert Smirke (1780-1867), Sydney Smirke (1798-1877), Sir John Taylor (1833-1912), Sir John Burnet (1859-1938), John Russell Pope (1874-1937) and Sir Colin St John Wilson. The latest addition to this largely distinguished group is Sir Norman Foster. In many instances their imprint remains, resplendent; in others (Puget, Hooke, Saunders) it has been buried beneath the present building, but plans survive of what once existed.

BLOOMSBURY

Bloomsbury, the part of London in which the Museum has always been situated, lies some distance outside the walls of the old City of London but not far from the seventh- to ninth-century Anglo-Saxon trading and residential settlement of Ludenwic, which was centred on the Strand and Covent Garden.

Prehistoric man wandered through the area, dropping axes; a few Roman coins and other objects have been found, and a Roman road ran nearby. It seems likely that modern Bloomsbury formed the southern part of the Anglo-Saxon estate of Tottenhale, the precursor of Tottenham

Court Estate. The 'Berewic' (an outlying part of an estate), as it was then known, had been bought from King Ethelred by the monks of Westminster Abbey. By the late twelfth century it had come into the hands of John Becointe, who in 1201 sold it to William Blemond. It is from Blemond that we derive the name Blemondsbury, or Bloomsbury.

The land remained in the Blemond family until they forfeited it in the 1260s after being involved in the barons' revolt against Henry III. There ensued a century of changing ownership followed by 140 years of stability under the Carthusian monastery at Smithfield until Henry VIII's Dissolution of the Monasteries. Henry subsequently gave the land to his Chancellor, Thomas Wriothesley, later 1st Earl of Southampton. Despite a brief confiscation in 1601, the land remained with the family until the death of the 4th Earl in 1667. During the English Civil War (1640-49) London declared for Parliament and a 10½-mile-long (17 km) rampart and ditch defence against Royalist forces encircled not only the City, but also Westminster and Southwark and much open country in between. The ditch passed approximately across the centre of the site which would be occupied by the Museum.

Having no male heir, the 4th Earl's property was willed to his three daughters and divided between them by the drawing of lots. His daughter Rachel, from his first marriage, inherited the Bloomsbury property, including Southampton House, built in 1660 and located to the north of what is now Bloomsbury Square. In 1669 Rachel married William Russell, afterwards Duke of Bedford, thereby bringing the area into the eventual control of the Bedford family.

Rachel's half-sister Elizabeth, from the Earl's second marriage, first married the Earl of Northumberland. On his death she married Ralph Montagu, afterwards Duke of Montagu, who was to build Montagu House, the first home of the British Museum. Ralph Montagu, born in 1638, son of the 3rd Baron Montagu of Boughton, had a career which was described as 'long and treacherous even by Reformation standards', while Jonathan Swift called him 'as arrant a knave as any in his time'. Montagu was Master of the Horse to the Duchess of York and Queen Catherine, and Ambassador Extraordinary to the Court of Louis XIV of France in 1669, 1676 and 1677. Despite occasional setbacks, he prospered under Charles II and James II and then managed to ingratiate himself with William III after the 'Glorious Revolution' of 1688, being created Duke of Montagu in 1705. The *DNB* commented, 'If Montagu was perfectly unscrupulous in obtaining money, he at least knew how to spend his wealth with dignity.' The most evident symbol of this was the palatial Montagu House.

The Southampton estate which passed to the Bedfords has been largely preserved to this day; however, on 19 June 1675 a piece of the land was relinquished, although at the time it was still kept in the family, as William Russell and his wife Rachel conveyed to her brother-in-law Ralph Montagu for £2,610 a plot of ground to the west of their own mansion, namely: 'all that peice [*sic*] or parcel of land lying in a feild commonly called or knowne by the name of Babers Feild, situate, lying and being in the Parish of St Giles in the Feilds containing by admeasurement seaven acres and twenty perches, now inclosed, separated or divided from the rest of the feild by a brick wall.' Montagu undertook that if he built on this space it would be: 'one faire and large messuage and dwelling house, fitt for him . . . and his family, to inhabitt, composed of an uniforme building together with all convenient stables, coach-houses, and other out offices suitable to the said mansion or dwelling house.'

MONTAGU HOUSE

Montagu selected as his architect the versatile genius Robert Hooke, astronomer, natural philospher and mechanic, Curator of Experiments and afterwards Fellow and Secretary of the Royal Society. Hooke worked closely with Christopher Wren on the rebuilding of London after the Great Fire of 1666, and it is believed that Wren advised on the work at Bloomsbury. Plans for the building had already been prepared when, on 11 February 1676, Montagu's wife wrote to her half-sister: 'If our house went up as fast as we have models made, we should be in it before you get to yours, for we have no less than three that are big enough for Miss Ann [her small daughter] to walk in.' The house's progress is confirmed by an entry in the diary of John Evelyn (1620-1706) on 11 May 1676, when he wrote, 'dined with Mr Charleton, and

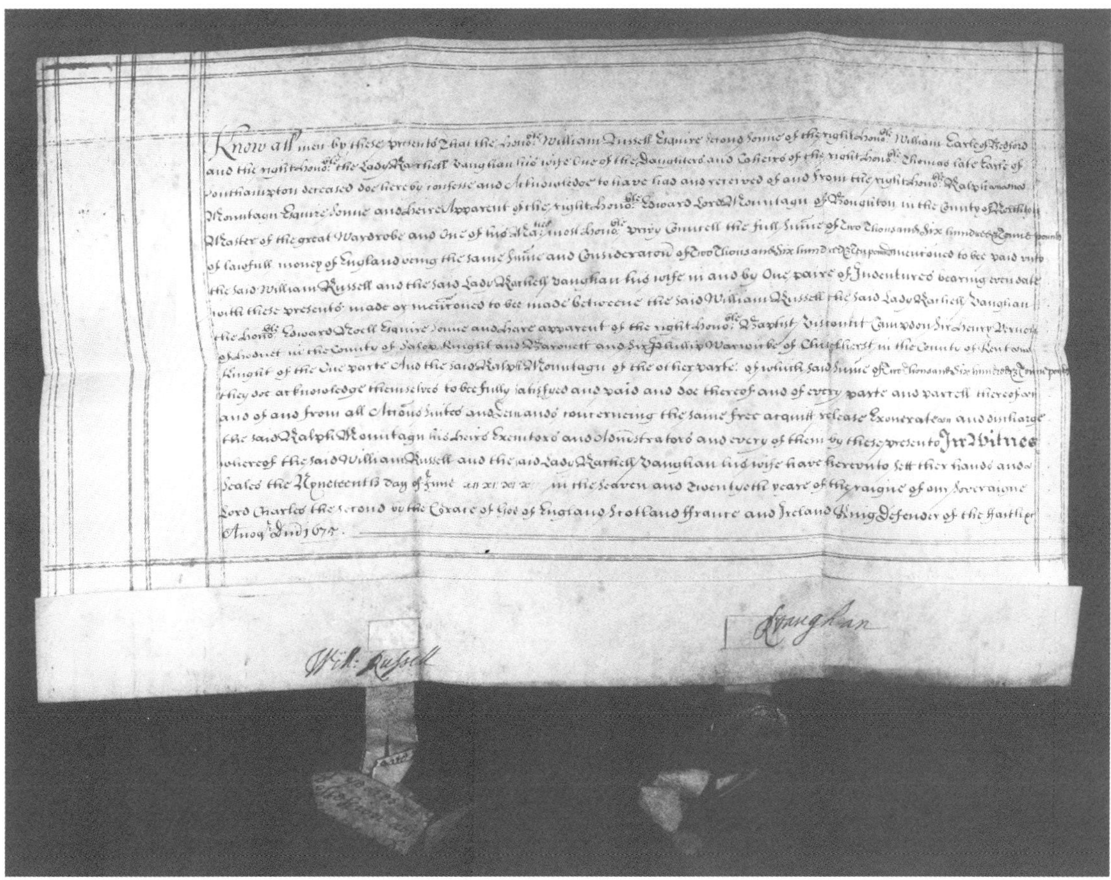

Know all men by these presents that the hon.ble William Russell Esquire second sonne of the right hon.ble William Earle of Bedford and the right hon.ble the Lady Rachell Vaughan his wife One of the Daughters and Coheires of the right hon.ble Thomas late Earle of Southampton deceased doe hereby confesse and Acknowledge to have had and received of and from the right hon.ble Ralph Mountagu Esquire sonne and heire Apparent of the right hon.ble Edward Lord Mountagu of Boughton in the County of Northton Master of the great Wardrobe and One of his Ma.ties most hon.ble privy Councell the full summe of Two Thousand Six hundred & tenne pounds of lawfull money of England being the same summe and Consideracon of Two Thousand Six hundred & tenne pounds mencioned to bee paid unto the said William Russell and the said Lady Rachell Vaughan his wife in and by One paire of Indentures bearing even date with these presents made or mencioned to bee made betweene the said William Russell the said Lady Rachell Vaughan the hon.ble Edward Noell Esquire sonne and heire apparent of the right hon.ble Baptist Viscount Campden Sir Henry Vernon of Hodnett in the County of Salop Knight and Baronett and Sir Phillip Warwicke of Chislehurst in the County of Kent Knight of the One parte And the said Ralph Mountagu of the other parte: of which said summe of Two Thousand Six hundred & tenne pounds they doe acknowledge themselves to bee fully satisfyed and paid and doe thereof and of every parte and parcell thereof and of and from all Accions suites and demands concerning the same free acquitt release Exonerate and discharge the said Ralph Mountagu his heires Executors and Administrators and every of them by these presents In Witnes whereof the said William Russell and the said Lady Rachell Vaughan his wife have hereunto sett their hands and Seales the Nyneteenth day of June in the seaven and Twentyeth yeare of the raigne of our Soveraigne Lord Charles the second by the Grace of God of England Scotland France and Ireland King Defender of the faith &c Anno Dni 1675.

Will: Russell

R Vaughan

1. *Receipt from William Russell and his wife, Rachel, for monies received (£2,610) from the sale of Babers Field to Ralph Montagu on 19 June 1675. Montagu House was subsequently built on this land.*

went to see Mr Montague's new palace, neare Bloomsbury, built by Mr Hooke of our Society, after the French manner.'

But this was only the first Montagu House, for Montagu's splendid palace survived for barely a decade. On the night of 19-20 January 1686 there was a great commotion in Bloomsbury. A letter to Mr Ellis, Secretary for the Revenue in Ireland relates:

> On Wednesday at one in the Morning a sad Fire happened at Montague House in Bloomsbury occasioned by the Steward's curing some Hangings etc in expectation of My Lord Montague's return home; and sending afterwards a woman to see that the Fire-pans with Charcoal were removed, which she told him she had done, though she never came there.

Lady Russell was at Southampton House and provided an eyewitness description in a letter written a few days later to her friend Dr Fitzwilliam:

> If you have heard of the dismal accident in the neighbourhood, you will easily believe Tuesday night was not a quiet one with us. About 1 o'clock in the night I heard a great noise in the Square, so little ordinary I called up a servant and sent her down to learn the occasion. She brought up a very sad one, that Montague House was on fire, and it was so indeed, it burnt with so great violence the whole house was consumed by 5 o'clock. The wind blew strong this way, so that we lay under fire a great part of the time, the sparks and flames continually covering the house and filling the court. My boy awaked and said he was almost stifled with smoke, but being told the reason would see it, and so was satisfied without fear.

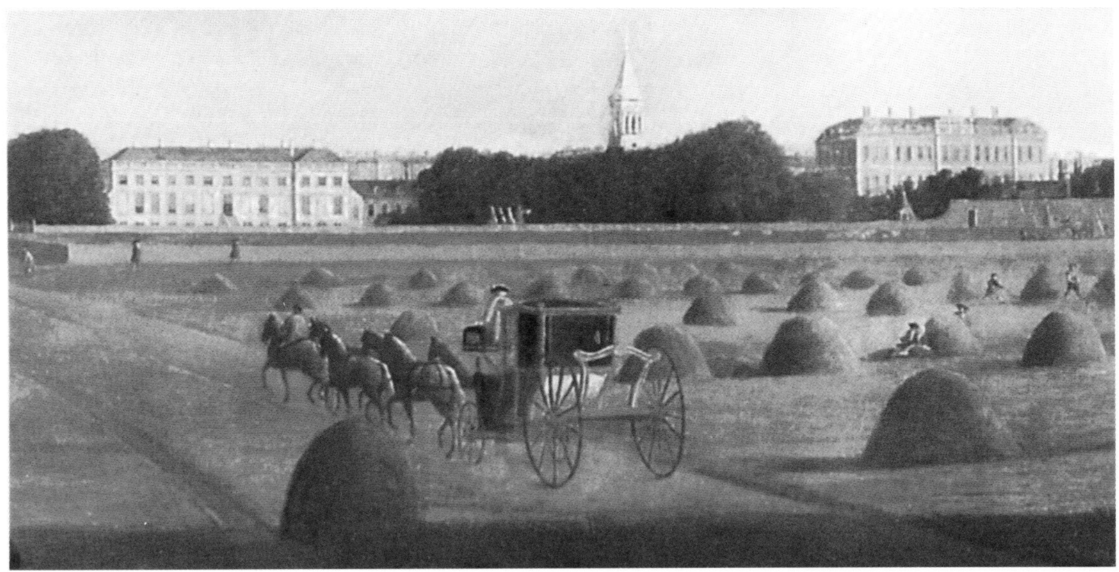

2. *This late eighteenth-century painting by Thomas Malton shows Montagu House (to the right), Southampton House (since demolished) and, beyond the trees, St George's Church (built by Nicholas Hawksmoor in 1731). Rural Bloomsbury was soon to disappear as the Duke of Bedford released land for development. In 1800 the hayfields were replaced by the formal gardens of Russell Square, laid out by Humphry Repton.*

The Earl of Devonshire's family was living in Montagu House at the time, Montagu having lent or let it to him. There followed a law suit against Devonshire which Montagu lost, but this does not seem to have overly affected his finances, for he

> . . . was oblig'd to bear the loss, and rebuild his House himself; in doing which, it was observable, that the first Model was so exquisitely perfect; that no Alteration could be made to Advantage; but the House was exactly built in the figure it had before.

Few images survive of the first Montagu House, although from Morgan's map of London (1682) the general form of the street frontage as well as the main wing can be seen to be almost identical to the appearance of the house after the fire. But was the building completely destroyed, as often reported, or was it the interior that was consumed by the flames? The service wings and gatehouse survived relatively intact. It seems unlikely that the mansion would have been flattened and the site cleared of all the remains, and recent archaeological investigation by the Museum has so far revealed no evidence of charred deposits, indicating that perhaps it was largely the interior which suffered.

The French influence on the new building was even more pronounced, although Montagu's second architect has not been positively identified. Horace Walpole, in his *Anecdotes of Painting* (1786), wrote: 'Monsieur Pouget, a French architect, conducted the building of Montagu House in 1678 [*sic*].' It has been suggested that this was the architect Pierre Puget, who was responsible for buildings in Toulon and Marseilles, but this seems unlikely on stylistic grounds. Another recent suggestion is that it was his brother Gaspard.

The new Montagu House is generally described in topographical books as the finest private house in London. Visitors gazed in awe at the grand staircase painted by Charles de la Fosse (1636-1716), the subject being, as a description of the house rather quaintly put it, 'Phaeton requesting Apollo to permit him to drive his chariot for a day' (col. pl. 1). Other rooms, too, were richly decorated, and in a vestibule on the upper floor was a ceiling painted with the Fall of Phaeton. The other painters employed were Jacques Rousseau (1631-91), who was reponsible for the landscape backgrounds and *trompe l'oeil*, and Jean-Baptiste Monnoyer (1634-99), who was particularly renowned for his flower paintings.

The house consisted of a series of buildings surrounding a quadrangular court. To the north was the main house (168 feet long and 57 feet high; 51 x 17 m) reached by steps from a courtyard. In wings to the east and west were offices, stables and other rooms. These wings were pierced by doorways decorated with Ionic pilasters on each side and a plain pediment. On the south, fronting Great Russell Street, was an arched entrance in a high, rather forbidding brick wall; above this an octangular turret surmounted by a largely wooden cupola. Inside, an Ionic colonnade extended the length of the south side of the courtyard.

Ralph Montagu's first wife died in 1690 and two years later he married the 'very mad' Elizabeth, Dowager Duchess of Albemarle. The Duke's first marriage had been described as 'lucky' (his first wife had been worth £6,000 a year) and no doubt the Dowager Duchess's £7,000 a year (inherited from her father the 2nd Duke of Newcastle) added to her attractions. She appears to have been distinctly odd, for a biographer recounted that the widowed Duchess was determined to give her hand to nobody but a sovereign prince. The scheming Montagu obliged by posing as the Emperor of China.

Ralph Montagu died at Montagu House in 1709. He was succeeded by his son John (1688-1749) as 2nd Duke. John is said to have lived in only one of the wings till he moved elsewhere, perhaps because the 'Empress of China' was still determinedly in residence. The area became a haunt of highwaymen – the Empress's carriage was ambushed in Great Russell Street one night in January 1750. In the fields behind were said to have occurred 'scenes of robbery, murder and every species of wickedness of which the heart can think'.

The 2nd Duke died in 1749 'at his House in Privy Garden', Westminster, leaving two daughters and co-heirs, Isabella and Mary, who also married well – Isabella to the 2nd Duke of Manchester and after his death to Sir Edward Hussey-Montagu, afterwards Earl of Beaulieu, and Mary to the 4th Earl of Cardigan. The once glittering Montagu House fell empty. There was a project in 1739-40 to turn it into a Foundling Hospital, but this came to nothing.

THE ORIGINS OF THE BRITISH MUSEUM

The origins of the British Museum lie in the collections of Sir Hans Sloane (1660-1753), a fashionable physician. Sloane, who succeeded Sir Isaac

3. *The second Montagu House of 1686. The print bears the inscription 'The elevation of Montagu House to the Court in Great Russell Street London is most humbly inscribed to his Grace the Duke of Montagu &c...by M. Pouget.' Horace Walpole wrote, 'What it wants in grace and beauty, is compensated by the spaciousness and lofty magnificence of the apartments'* (Anecdotes of Painting, *1786).*

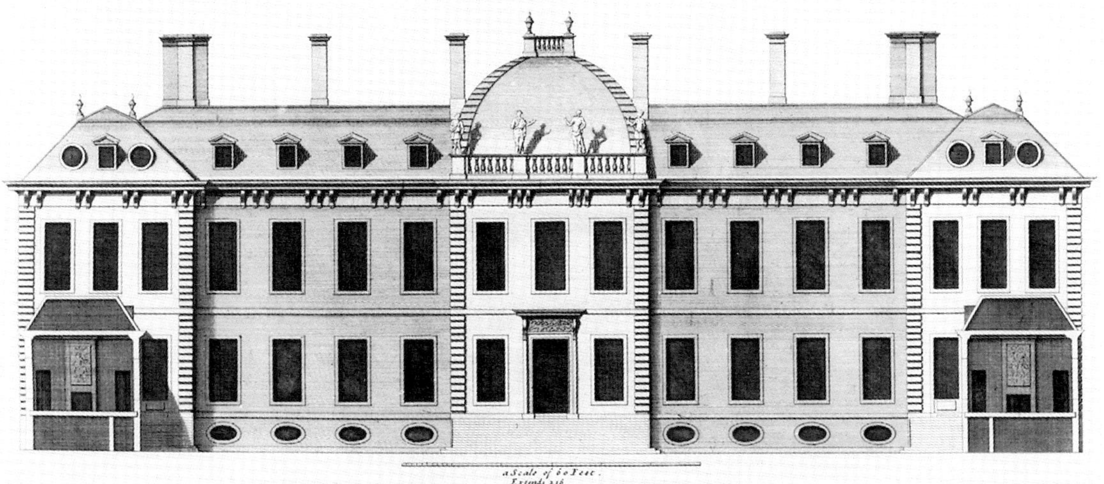

Newton as President of the Royal Society, had, like many of his contemporaries, an intense interest in natural history. The seventeenth century being a small world, Sloane was already linked to Montagu House by his appointment in 1688 as physician to the the 2nd Duke of Albemarle (1653-88), who had been newly appointed Governor of Jamaica. The time in Jamaica provided Sloane with the opportunity to amass a remarkable natural history collection. He was less successful with his patient, for the Duke, whose lifestyle was inappropriate to the climate, died within nine months, it having been suggested that his unfortunate disposition to 'being merry' was partly due to the effect of the Duchess, whose 'wayward and peevish temper made him frequently think a bottle a much more desirable companion'. On arriving back in England in 1689, Sloane continued in the employment of the mad Dowager Duchess for four years. As his career prospered, he moved to No. 3 Great Russell Street, a short distance east of Montagu House, and continued to collect obsessively, eventually expanding into No. 4. By the time of his death he had moved to the manor house at Chelsea and his collection of around 80,000 objects (natural history, antiquities and artificial curiosities, coins, prints, books, manuscripts), plus a large herbarium, was one of the wonders of London.

Not wishing to see his beloved collection broken up, Sloane appointed an influential group of Trustees to oversee the provisions of his will, by which his 'museum' was offered on first refusal to King George II for the British nation in return for the payment of £20,000 to his two daughters. Should the nation turn the offer down, the will provided for the collection to go abroad. The King had little interest – as so often, the Treasury was bare – but Parliament, particularly Speaker Arthur Onslow, was determined that the Sloane collection should not be lost. After some careful manoeuvring, in June 1753 the British Museum Act received the royal assent. This provided for funds to be raised by a public lottery for the purchase of Sloane's collection and the collection of manuscripts brought together by the Harleys, Earls of Oxford (which was available for purchase, the books having already been disposed of), and for a suitable repository. The collection of manuscripts amassed by the Cotton family, which the nation had had since 1700 but had not quite known what to do with, was also made over to the Museum. A new body of Trustees headed, *ex officio*, by the Archbishop of Canterbury, the Lord Chancellor and the Speaker of the House of Commons, was appointed to oversee the national interest, for this was the first of a new type of museum which was to become a model for others, a collection no longer in private, royal or church hands, but which belonged to the people. The Trustees, a 'body corporate', have maintained this continuing responsibility to Parliament and the nation to the present day.

THE BRITISH MUSEUM AT MONTAGU HOUSE – EARLY YEARS

The Trustees of the newly established British Museum found themselves possessed of a moderate sum (£95,194 8*s*. 2*d*.) in dubiously conducted lottery money and a large collection requiring a home. Somewhat fortuitously this was a tripartite collection – library, natural history, antiquities – but this was in keeping with the universal ideals of the time. The history of the Museum and its building consists in part of the attempt, eventually unsuccessful, to cling to the wide-ranging ideals of its founders.

On 13 February 1754 the Trustees had before them two proposals, one from the husbands of the Montagu heiresses, the Earl of Cardigan and Sir Edward Montagu, who offered Montagu House for £10,000, and the other from Charles Sheffield, who wished to sell Buckingham House (later to become Buckingham Palace) 'with the gardens and field' for £30,000. The first of very many Committees to do with the Museum building was established to consider the matter. At a meeting on 3 April the offer of Buckingham House was rejected on account of 'the Greatness of the sum demanded for it, the inconvenience of the situation, and other circumstances'. Before finally deciding on Montagu House the Trustees considered a scheme to build a museum in Old Palace Yard, as part of a plan for new Houses of Parliament and other public offices. Since it was estimated that this would cost £50,000-£60,000, the idea was quickly abandoned. Another suggestion – the conversion of the Banqueting House in Whitehall – appears to have been floated but not formally considered, for in 1756 one of the

Museum's surveyors (a Mr Vardy) received £84 for producing drawings to show how this might be done.

A surveyors' report on Montagu House was obtained on 22 February 1754. The surveyors were rather enthusiastic, and 'represented it as a substantial well-built brick building, the foundation sound, and free from any material cracks or settlement . . . roof sound . . . proper and convenient for the purposes of a Museum.' They did recommend removal of the turret and cupola over the gateway as 'being impossible to repair'. (This, ironically, was the last part of Montagu House to be taken down, almost a century later: see p. 28) On 11 April 1754 eleven Trustees met at Montagu House and took advice from the architect Theodore Jacobson (d.1771), one of the trustees of Sloane's will and designer of the Foundling Hospital, as to how the rooms on the upper floor might be extended for Museum purposes. Articles of Agreement were executed on 3 June 1754 and the purchase was completed on 5 April 1755 at a cost of £10,250.

The Museum inherited a magnificent volume of plans of Montagu House (col. pl. 2) executed by Henry Flitcroft (1697-1769), who from a lowly beginning and an apprenticeship as a joiner had by 1720 risen through patronage and considerable talent to become architectural assistant to the 3rd Earl of Burlington (1695-1763). The Earl, a generous patron of the arts, is believed to have noticed his drawing skills by chance and set about nurturing them to their mutual advantage.

The house had been empty for a number of years and was not in good repair. Also, the surveyors had been over-optimistic. As is not unknown with old buildings, even before the Museum was thrown open to the public more money (£12,000) had been spent on repairs and fittings than had been paid for the actual purchase. The Trustees may have miscalculated the amount of money they would have to spend on repairs and alterations (£50,000 over the next half century), but their miscalculation as to the future scope of their collections was monumentally wrong and in particular failed to predict the accession of large stone antiquities which would eventually prove too much for the floors.

The Harleian manuscripts moved in at the end of May and the beginning of June 1755, the Sloane library and Cottonian collection in July 1755, the Edwards library in August 1755 and the Sloane museum at the beginning of December. Staff, headed by a 'Principal Librarian' (a title which indicated the relative predominance of the library as compared to natural history and antiquities), were appointed in 1756.

Miss Catherine Talbot (1721-70) wrote a long letter to Mrs Anne Berkeley (the widow of Bishop Berkeley, the philosopher) describing a visit to London in August 1756. Remarking that the weather is 'cool and fair', and adding 'I must not omit to tell you that I am grown Fat, and have been suspected of putting on Rouge', Miss Talbot gives a glimpse of the Museum prior to its official opening (British Library, Add. MS. 39311, f.82):

> One Evening we spent at Montague House, henceforth to be known by the name of the British Musaeum. I was delighted to see Science in this Town so Magnificently & Elegantly lodged; perhaps You have seen that fine House & Pleasant Garden: I never did before, but thought I liked it much better now, inhabited by Valuable Mss, Silent Pictures, & Ancient Mummies, than I should have done when it was filled with Miserable Fine People, a Seat of Gayety on the inside, & a place of Duels without . . . Nothing is yet ranged but two or three rooms of Mss. Three & Thirty Rooms in all are to be filled with Curiosities of every kind. A number of Learned & Deserving Persons are made happy by the places bestowed on them to preserve & show this fine Collection: These have Comfortable Apartments in the Wings, & a Philosophic Grove and Physick Garden open to the view of a delightful Country, where at leisure hours they may improve their health & their Studies together.

The Museum opened to visitors on 15 January 1759. On the first floor were the Cottonian and Harleian libraries, the Sloane manuscripts, medals, most of the antiquities, and Sloane's natural history. On the lower floor were the Royal library given by George II in 1757 and the Sloane and Edwards libraries. Changes were made as the collections grew. The Otaheite Room with its neat mosaic pattern wallpaper (opened in 1778) housed collections acquired on Captain Cook's round-the-world voyages – a display comparable to today's moon dust. Somewhat cowed visitors were admitted in small groups, initially under the con-

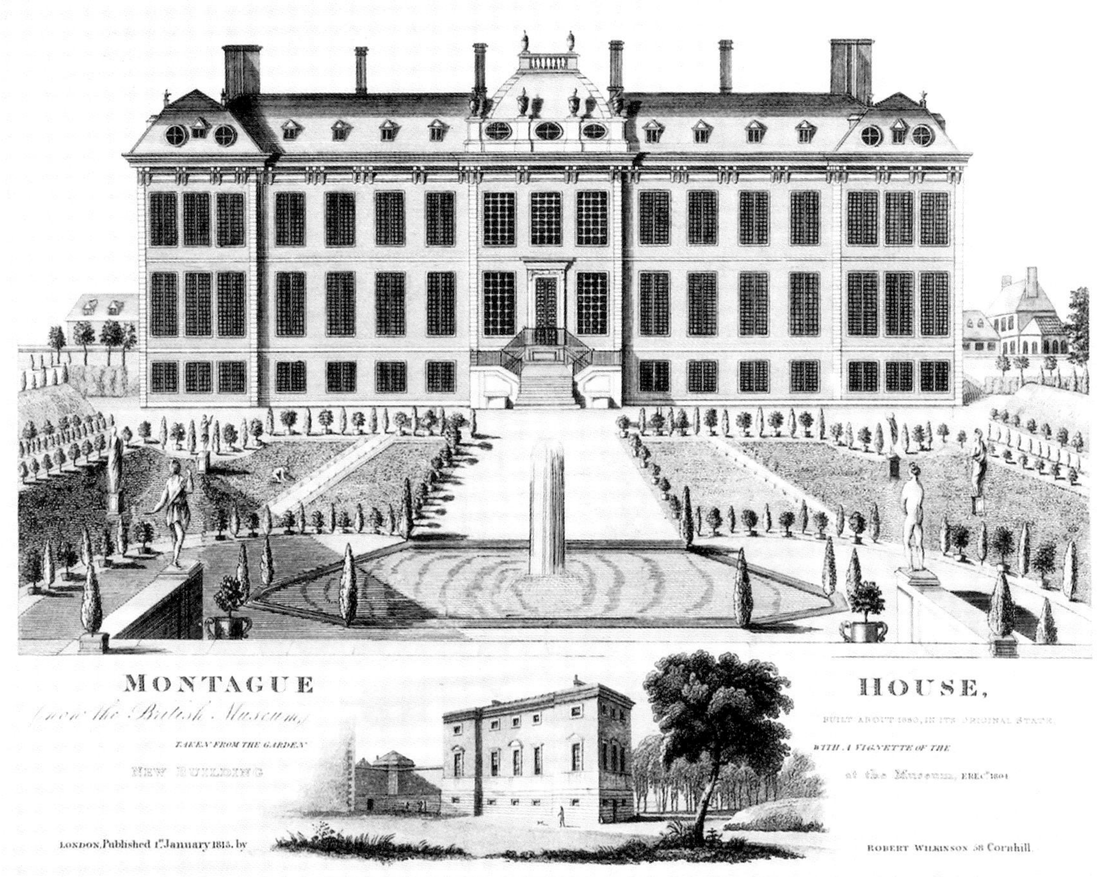

4. *A print of 1813 shows the north façade of Montagu House 'in its original state' and its formally laid out gardens, soon to disappear. Below is a vignette of the Townley Gallery built on the western side of the gardens.*

trol of a guide, their visit circumscribed. Typically, the 1808 *Synopsis* (guide-book) remarked: 'The first floor consisting of twelve rooms, contains the Library of Printed Books. Strangers are not conducted through these apartments, as the mere sight of the outside of books cannot convey either instruction or amusement.'

Within two years an increasingly liberal attitude towards visitors resulted in the admission of 'all persons of decent appearance without limitation of numbers' to the galleries, where they were allowed to roam at will.

THE GARDENS OF MONTAGU HOUSE

At least until they began to fill up with sheds to store the growing collections, the gardens of Montagu House were the Trustees' great pride and joy. Montagu's garden had been laid out in the style of the time in large grass plots and gravelled paths, ornamented with pieces of sculpture, with a raised terrace skirting the three sides (north, west and east). By the time of its acquisition by the Museum, the garden was in a state of neglect and was combed by anthills. These were cut and carried away at the rate of two shillings per hundred and the garden was taken in hand. By the end of 1755 it was reported that: 'The whole garden has been mowed, weeded, and cleared of the Anthills; the Gravel Walks and borders restored, the Slopes made less steep and together with the borders planted; the Kitchen Garden [in an additional piece of land held on lease] trenched; a Tool House built in it; and the Basin repaired.' In the summer of 1756 an agreement was made with Mr Bramley, the gardener, for 'Rolling, Mowing, Watering, Planting, Digging, Pruning the Trees', the Trustees to provide 'Trees, Plants, Seeds, Dung and Gravel'. By the end of the century the garden contained no fewer than 600 species of plants, all in a flourishing state.

The gardens were first opened to visitors on 11 March 1757. In 1762 it was found necessary to issue annual admission tickets in order to restrict numbers. In 1769 admission was allowed from 7 a.m. to half an hour after sunset, and the porter was to 'warn all persons previously with a handbell to leave the gardens at that time'. A Victorian Principal Librarian wrote: 'Let not such small records be accounted trivial. The vision of the porter and his handbell ringing out the loiterers under the glowing twilight of a summer evening is one to be cherished by dwellers in the crowded and fog-ridden Bloomsbury of the present day.'

The fine houses in Great Russell Street were replaced with smaller dwellings and in 1799 the Duke of Bedford offered building leases to the north of the Museum. The Trustees were unable to acquire land from the Duke but they did insist on preserving their former right of way out of the Museum, 'for walking into and taking ayre in the feilds', which ran via a footpath 20 feet (6 m) wide leading out of the north gate through the midst of the new houses.

The garden was submerged beneath Smirke's new building.

MONTAGU HOUSE – REPAIR AND MAINTENANCE

In 1754 the Trustees appointed Henry Keene (1726–76) principal architect and surveyor with responsibility for surveying and restoring the recently purchased Montagu House. Keene's task was not an easy one, especially as he was a busy private architect and, until his death, was also surveyor to Westminster Abbey. Montagu House was beset with damp, which was entering from all directions. Repairs to the roof caused additional damage to the fine frescoes during a long spell of unexpected rain. For twenty-one years Keene supervised the shoring up of the old house in an attempt to receive the expanding collections and meet the needs of the staff in residence. Metal and wooden ceiling supports were cleverly disguised as bookcases; stables were converted into staff apartments; windows, chimneys and cellars were altered to reduce the risk of fire.

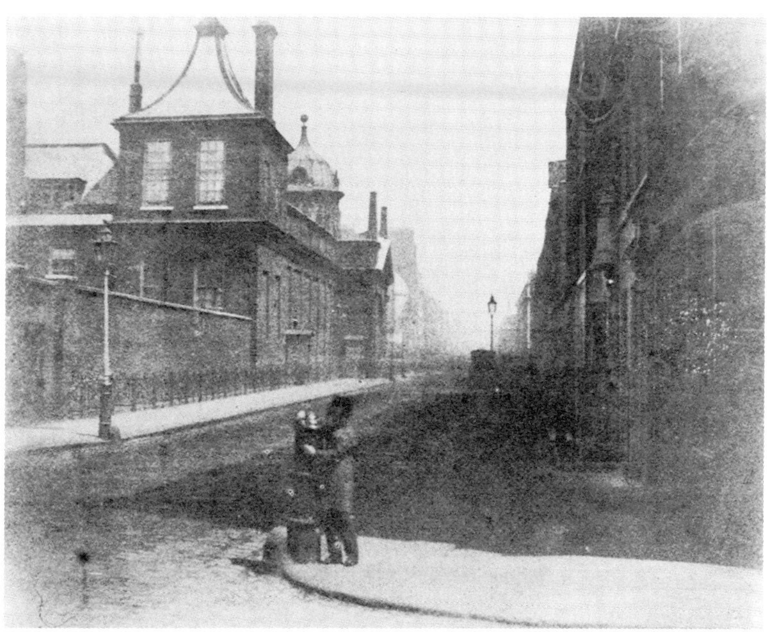

5. *Photograph of Montagu House and Great Russell Street taken by John Muir Wood from the south-west around 1843. Within ten years this view had altered beyond recognition.*

On Keene's death in 1776 his rescue work was continued for a short time by James Wyatt (1746–1813), a successful young architect who also took over Keene's work at Westminster Abbey. Wyatt secured his reputation some four years earlier with his sensitive alterations to the old Pantheon in Oxford Street. This was somewhat removed from his first Museum assignments, where he might be asked to redesign a bookcase or undertake alterations to the Principal Librarian's 'necessary'.

During the last quarter of the eighteenth century the ongoing reconstruction and repair were increasingly delegated to various assistant surveyors (John Gorham was particularly active). However, from 1792 Wyatt's nephew Jeffry Wyatt (later Wyattville, 1766–1840) was assigned various projects at the Museum. In 1799 Jeffry entered into a successful partnership with John Armstrong, a Pimlico builder, and together they continued their association with the Museum.

Thus Montagu House gradually deteriorated. Visits could be hazardous as pieces of the building had an increasing tendency to drop off. Dry rot was first reported in 1766. The following year one of the weights in the clock fell through the floor of the Clock Room down on to the colonnade and shattered one of the lamps fixed in the gateway. In 1780 the stone vases over the colonnade had to be removed, one having fallen and damaged a gentleman's carriage.

PAYING FOR THE BUILDING

Almost from the beginning the Trustees were beset by anxieties over funding. A single year's experience demonstrated that it was impossible for them to meet the expenses of the Museum with the modest income of £900 from their invested capital of £30,000. The Government's hope had been that the Museum would be self-supporting. In 1760 the Trustees first appealed to the Treasury, their expenses having exceeded income by £516. This had no effect, for the war with France was then at its height and money was scarce. The resources of the Trustees continued to dwindle and in 1762 all that remained was the invested sum of £30,000. A petition in February that year resulted in a grant for £2,000, the first of those that were to follow, at first periodically and then, from the beginning of the nineteenth century, annually. Apart from meagre private funds, the Trustees were henceforth dependent on Government for their funding. Thus future building works were to reflect an uneasy situation – the Treasury as paymasters, the Trustees responsible to the nation for their collections under Act of Parliament and, sandwiched in between, the architect. In June 1815 responsibility for the care of the building was taken out of the Trustees' hands and given to the Office of Works (a responsibility which its successors retained until 1 April 1988).

Worries about finance became increasingly acute with the vast increase in the collections, especially of antiquities, which was to come with the nineteenth century and for which the building was woefully inadequate. The first significant collection of antiquities (a warning of things to come) was Sir William Hamilton's collection of Greek vases, purchased in 1772.

THE TOWNLEY GALLERY

The arrival in 1802 of heavy Egyptian antiquities, including the Rosetta Stone and the sarcophagus of Nectanebo, acquired by the Crown under the Treaty of Alexandria and presented to the Museum, turned the Trustees' thoughts to the erection of a new building which would be rather more suitable than the sheds in the garden then housing the large pieces of sculpture that the floors could not support. In 1802 they formed a Committee to draw up a building programme for the future. This Committee (the first of many) consisted of Sir Joseph Banks (1743–1820), Sir William Hamilton (1730–1803), Thomas Astle (1735–1803) and Charles Townley (1737–1805, himself a noted collector), and reported in 1803. They had met repeatedly at Townley's house in Park Street, where his collection of classical sculpture was displayed and 'where they had abundant opportunities of studying the most approved methods of exhibiting works of sculpture to advantage'. Their main recommendation was that a new wing running northwards should be erected near the north-west angle of Montagu House and joined to it by passages concealed by a colonnade which could also be used for display.

Being of a somewhat practical turn of mind, they added:

> ... there will be, on the west side of the new building, a considerable space of ground, on which groups of Apartments, incapable of architectural regularity, and always disgusting in appearance, such as detached Rooms proper to receive fine Statues and other valuable Works of Art which require skylights and recesses of particular Shapes, to shew them properly, may be placed, so as to be wholly hid from the view, by the body of the new building.

This was somewhat prophetic, heralding a recurrent solution to the Trustees' problems as the collections continually expanded far beyond forecasts. In 1804 the Trustees successfully petitioned Parliament for money to meet the expense of the new building.

The architect of the Museum's first purpose-built gallery was George Saunders (1762-1839). Saunders, who at the age of eighteen designed a façade for the New Street Theatre in Birmingham, secured his reputation as an architect with his extension to Caen Wood, the Highgate residence of the 2nd Earl of Mansfield. He was subsequently, for twenty-eight years, Chairman of the Commission on Sewers (a testimony of his dedication to the 'system' at the Museum) and was appointed Surveyor for Middlesex.

There was some debate as to the preferred style of the new project. The Sub-Committee put forward alternative plans produced by Saunders, one elevation much in keeping with Montagu House, the other (which they preferred) plainer. Of the latter they wrote that,

> ... they have, in studying the harmony and proportion of its Character, carefully avoided all kind of expensive ornament, and ... have suited the general appearance of the outside to that of the old building, as far as they found themselves able, with a due regard to their ideas of good taste, and to the proper construction of a building intended for the express purpose of exhibiting Works of Art to advantage, and as much as in their opinion, the Architectural usage of this Country requires, in a building distinct from the principal Front.

Montagu House was now out of fashion, the Committee remarking: 'they seriously doubt whether the public will approve a nearer approximation to the style of the worst period of French architecture, in a house erected in 1676, and therefore likely to be rebuilt a Century at least before the new building will fail.'

Initially the main Board of Trustees decided that they preferred the elevation which reflected the style of the old house. However, following difficulties of construction, they reverted to the plainer elevation recommended by the Sub-Committee (col. pl. 3).

Drawings were prepared in 1803 and work began towards the end of 1804. The building was completed in 1808 at a cost of £28,144 12s. Although at first intended for Egyptian antiquities, the designs were altered to cope with Charles Townley's large collection of classical sculpture,

6. *The precursor of Sir Robert Smirke's courtyard design, showing the proposed extension of the Townley Gallery (west) and a parallel wing (east): a plan of c. 1803 by George Saunders.*

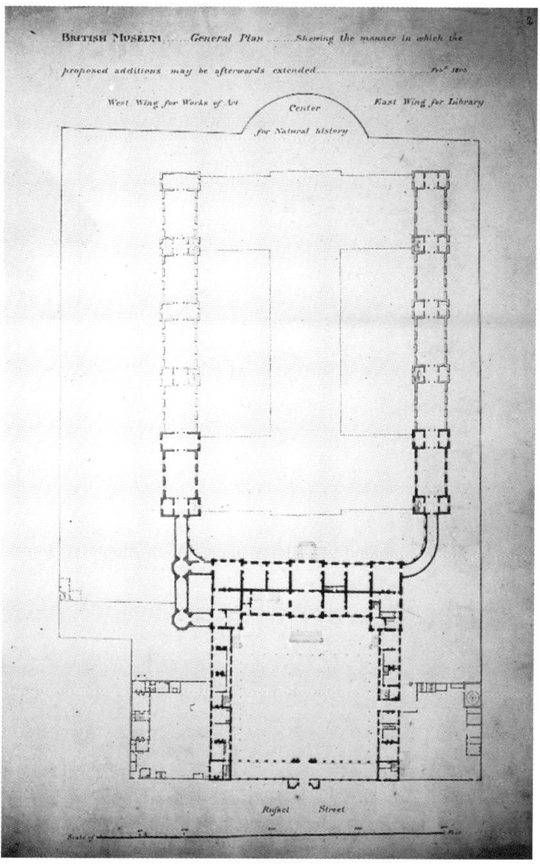

purchased by the Museum from his family after his death in 1805.

The Townley Gallery was opened with some pomp on 3 June 1808 by Queen Charlotte accompanied by the Dukes of Cumberland and Cambridge and four Princesses. The Trustees recorded the cost to the Museum: cold collation £29 10*s*. 0*d*., drugget (laid on the step and spoiled) £6 4*s*. 0*d*.

The Egyptian antiquities from the Townley Gallery were moved to the northern section of Robert Smirke's West Wing in 1834 and the classical sculptures were rearranged. When the gallery was demolished the classical material was transferred elsewhere in the Museum.

7. *The Temporary Elgin Room, which housed the Parthenon sculptures and Phigaleian marbles from 1817 until 1831.*

The Townley Gallery was partly demolished in winter 1842 and completely removed in December 1846 to allow completion of the southern section of the West Wing (now the Egyptian Sculpture Gallery); no visible trace remains.

Saunders, like his predecessors, was also reponsible for various minor projects such as, in 1806, finding a means of 'preventing nuisances against the street front of the British Museum'. His solution was to introduce iron bar railings, 'leaving an interval of about four feet [1.2 m] between the rail and the wall, and avoiding angles as much as possible'. The reinstatement of the Principal Librarian's 'deranged garden', in the way of the Townley Gallery, proved more of a problem. The Trustees appear to have taken pity on its owner, Mr Planta, and a compensatory greenhouse 'of glass lights' was provided for the princely sum of £33.

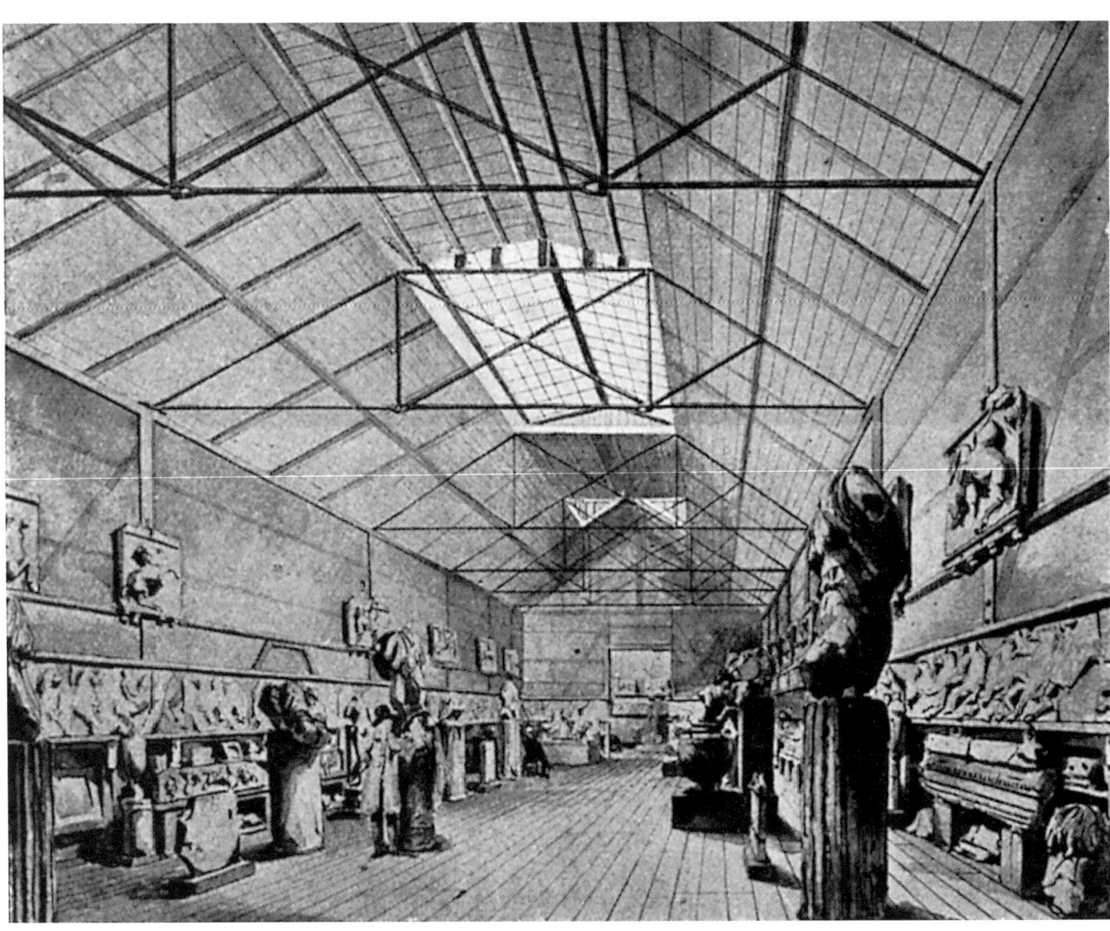

THE TEMPORARY ELGIN ROOM

In 1816 Lord Elgin's collection of sculptures from the Parthenon and other items was purchased by the British Government and deposited 'in perpetuity' in the British Museum by Act of Parliament. A temporary gallery, described as 'two spacious rooms on the ground floor', brick-built with a pine floor, the roof tied together with iron girders, was attached to the west side of the Townley Gallery at a cost of £1,700 and opened to the public on 3 February 1817. Also displayed here were the 'Phigaleian marbles', the sculptures from the temple of Apollo Epikourios at Bassae in Phigaleia, Greece, which had been acquired by the Museum in 1814, and other classical statuary. This was the first building designed for the Trustees by Robert Smirke (p. 35), one of the three Attached Architects of Works. For a temporary building it had a comparatively long life, demonstrating a later Principal Librarian's adage that 'what is temporary in a public building whose development is governed by Parliamentary grants, often [exhibits] a disposition to become permanent'.

The Temporary Elgin Room was demolished in 1831. No visible trace now remains, but a successful sale of the components of the dismantled room no doubt pleased the Treasury and assisted one or two speculative builders in the neighbourhood.

SIR ROBERT SMIRKE'S GREAT DESIGN

The Trustees' 1802 Committee had also submitted a more comprehensive development scheme. This envisaged a future extension of the West Wing northwards and the erection of another corresponding long wing on the eastern side of the garden. In the years following the completion of the Townley Gallery the collections continued to expand and Montagu House to deteriorate. By 1820 the Trustees were having to resort to propping up the floor of the Saloon with cast iron pillars and Smirke had again to consider the earlier suggestions. Their initial proposal, which echoed the original scheme, was for 'a [north-] eastwards extension of the Townley Gallery for the Athenian and Phigaleian Marbles' and the erection of a corresponding (eastern) wing for manuscripts and 'the more precious articles of natural history'. On 10 February 1821 the Trustees resolved to present a memorial to Government.

Perhaps unsurprisingly, the neighbours did not relish the view of a 295-foot-long, 60-foot-high building (90 x 18 m). In March 1821 formal notice was served on the Trustees by the Duke of Bedford requiring them to refrain from erecting buildings in their garden. Although the original conveyance of the land to Ralph Montagu had included the provision that no building should be erected on the north part of his land beyond the range of Southampton House, except summer houses or banqueting houses in the garden or 'what shall be for the inlargement of the great Mansion House', the Trustees won their case, having argued successfully that the neighbourhood was already spoiled by the streets and squares previously introduced by the Bedford Estates.

There is a tale that in 1823 King George IV, somewhat short of funds and having threatened to sell to the Russians his father's library of over 65,000 volumes and 19,000 unbound tracts, came to a secret arrangement with the Government that they should buy it in return for £50,000 siphoned from secret funds. No evidence has yet been found of any shady transaction, however, and it is thought probable that it was a scurrilous contemporary rumour put about some years later by Frederick, Duke of York (it emerged again in the *Quarterly Review* of December 1850). In any event, it was agreed that the books should go to the British Museum. A condition of the gift was that the King's library was to be kept 'entire and separate' from the rest of the Museum library 'in a Repository to be appropriated exclusively to that purpose'. A Parliamentary grant of £40,000 for the construction of a suitable building was the catalyst which sparked off the massive Museum rebuilding project.

As was the Trustees' practice, another Committee was established in June 1823. Plans by Sir Robert Smirke for the King's Library, which was to be part of a general design for the Museum, were approved on 11 July 1823. These provided for the erection of three sides of a quadrangle to the north of Montagu House, the fourth side to be constructed when the house itself was demolished.

Some controversy surrounds the dates of the general design and of the elevation of the south front, since Smirke's plans emerged piecemeal to

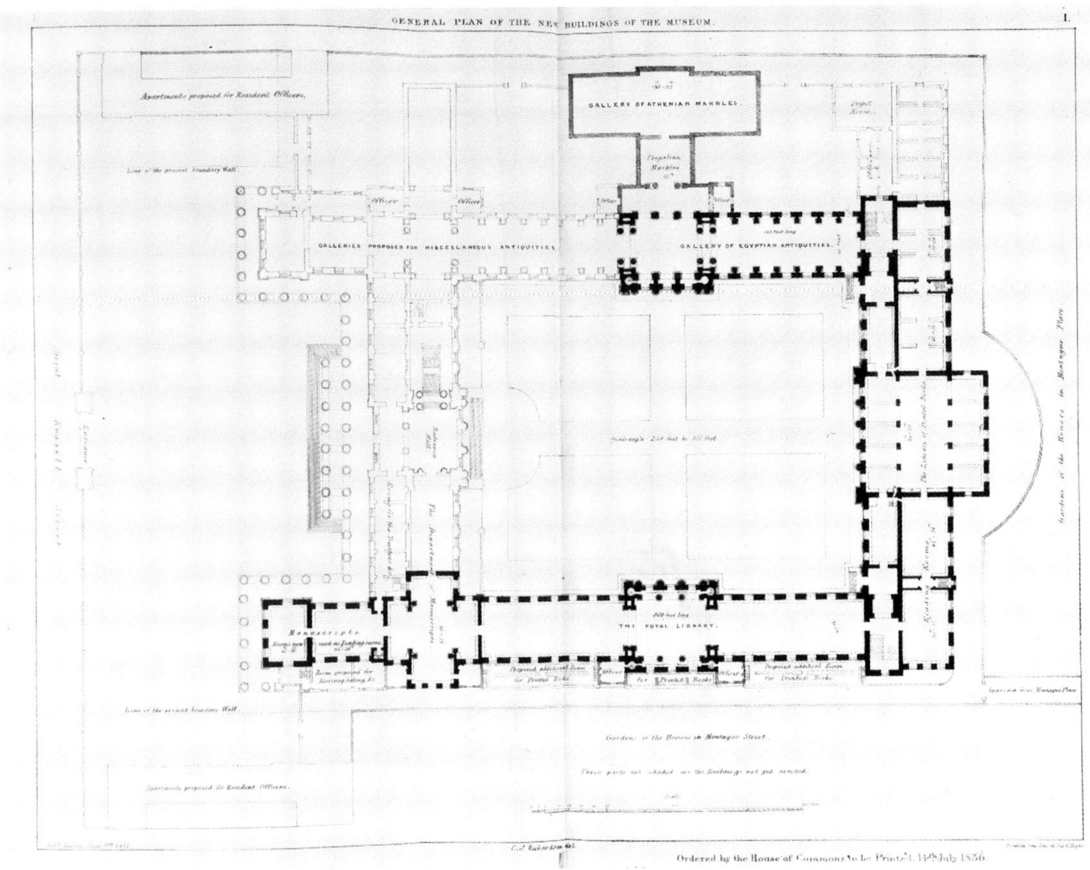

8. *An 1836 lithograph plan showing the work already completed and that proposed during the following decade. This was submitted to the House of Commons Select Committee on the British Museum of 1835-6.*

public notice. The general plan was not published until 1836, the front elevation in 1843. The basic quadrangular layout in the gardens was an obvious solution which would preserve space for the collections in Montagu House as the new building went up, and it echoed the 1803 proposals. It has, however, been suggested that the final design of the south front came later. The date is important, as it would indicate whether or not Smirke could, for example, have been influenced by Karl Friedrich Schinkel's Altes Museum in Berlin, which was designed in 1823 and built in 1825-8. A letter from Smirke to the Principal Librarian dated 12 December 1823 states only that:

> I regret very much that I am not prepared to comply with the wish which you say will be probably be expressed by the Trustees tomorrow to see a drawing of the design for the Principal Elevation of the Building to front Great Russell Street. A Design for this Elevation was submitted to the Lords of the Treasury with the other drawings and was approved subject to certain alterations but I have not yet made the drawing showing these Alterations, for knowing that this part of the Plan would not be carried into execution for many years, I did not consider the matter as urgent.

Plans and elevations for the whole of the building were shown to the Trustees on 10 June 1826 and 22 June 1826. At the latter meeting Smirke was directed to leave these with the Trustees, he being permitted to 'have the same home upon any occasion when it may be necessary to make alterations', such alterations to be noted on the drawings.

More detailed plans were approved in 1827. A model (now lost) was produced in 1831, 'prepared according to designs approved by the Treasury in 1825'. There were certainly some alterations, but as late as 1841 a Trustees Committee noted that in spite of the entreaties of the Keeper of Antiquities 'it was inadvisable to depart . . . from the general plan sanctioned in 1823'. Pevsner, in a 1953 article, thought that the design for the south front was later than 1823, but Mordaunt Crook adduces the compelling evidence of much earlier plans to contend that in 1821 work began on a general plan which was finished early in 1823 and that in its essentials this scheme remained unaltered.

Smirke's building is in the 'Greek Revival' style influenced by his travels and also the vogue for ancient Greece during the eighteenth and early nineteenth centuries. In contrast to the exuberance of Gothic architecture, it has been described as 'chaste and grand and truly classical'.

THE KING'S LIBRARY

The start of work on the King's Library (the East Wing) was witnessed on 14 July 1823 by one of the Museum's diarists – Thomas Conrath (d.1840), an attendant in the Elgin Gallery for some twenty years, who also noted:

> Monday, Septr 8th 1823 the first bricks were laid for the foundation of the new building at the British Museum near the east end of the old house, the ground being springy I saw the bricks and mortar laid in the water. The foundation is about twelve feet [3.6 m] deep . . . .

There was a delay caused by unusually heavy rainfall. The library was completed in 1827, the 65,000 books and 800 boxes of unbound pamphlets for which it was designed moved in in 1828, and the wing was virtually complete in 1830. Its immense size (300 ft long, general breadth 41 ft and height 31 ft; 91 x 12.5 x 9.5 m) required the innovative use of cast iron, and Smirke informed a Parliamentary Committee that the arched iron plates used 'were the first beams in London of so great length and large openings through the width

9. *The western elevation of the King's Library, Robert Smirke's East Wing (1823-8), the first phase of his quadrangular scheme: ' . . . a proper building for the reception of the Royal Library and a Picture Gallery over it, and for providing a fit place for the deposit of manuscripts, such building to form part of a general plan' (Minutes of the Trustees' General Meeting, 26 January 1823).*

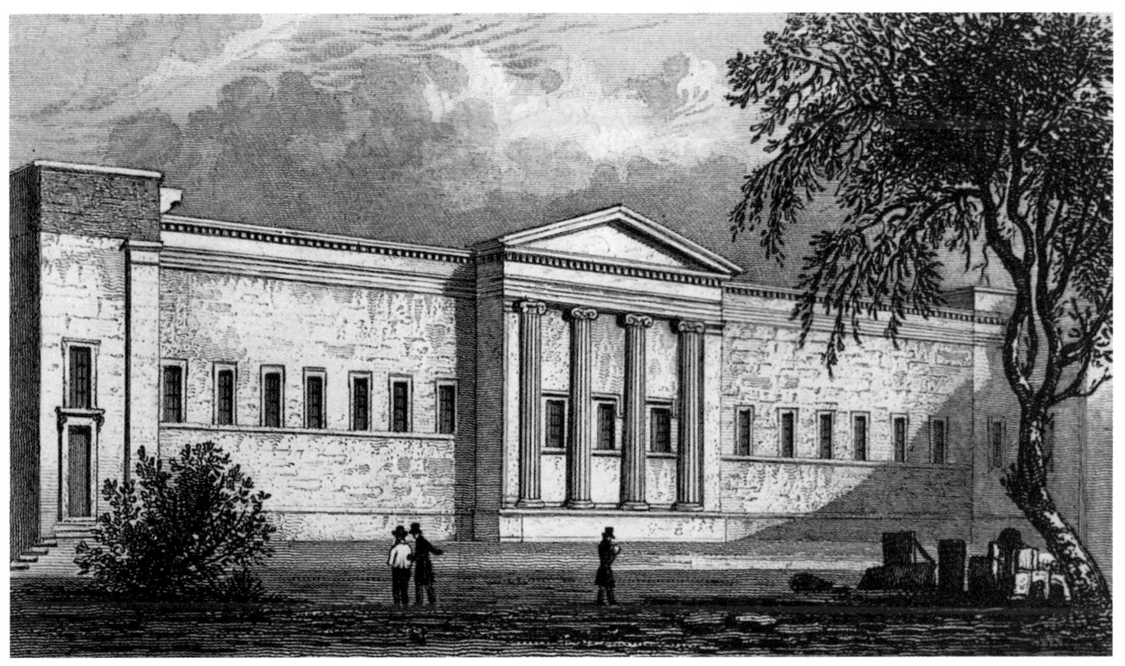

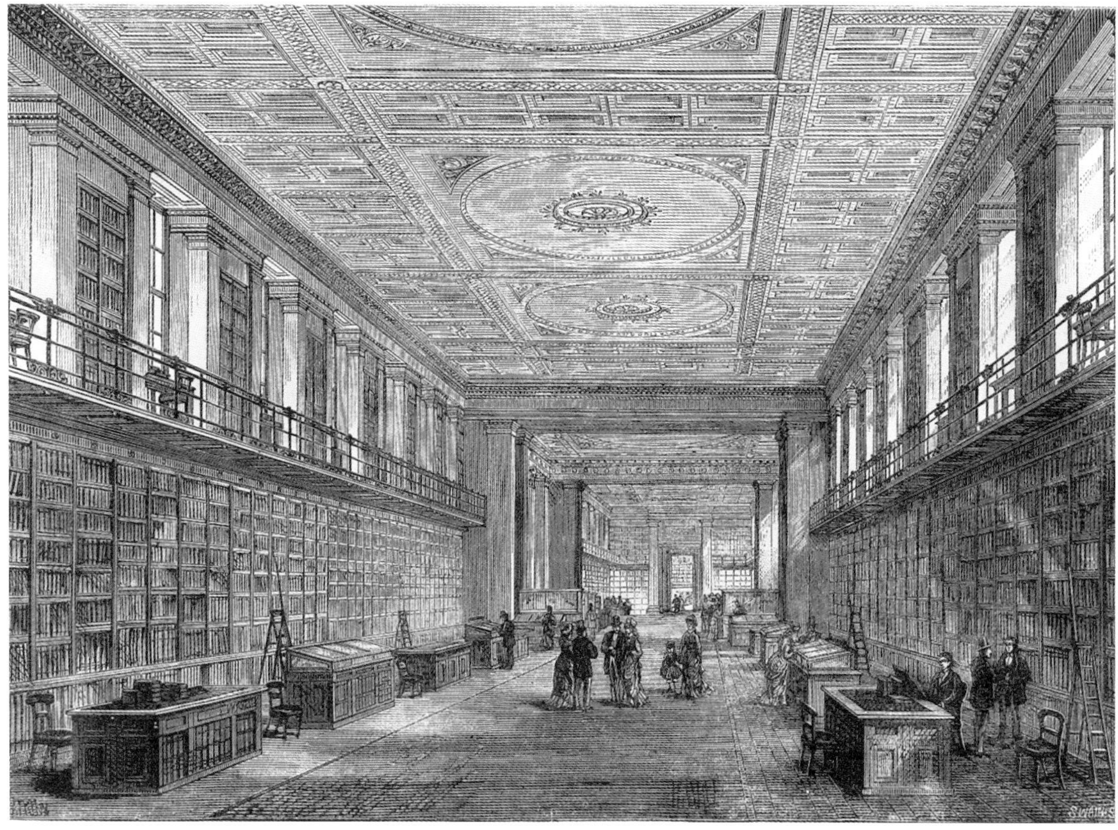

10. *This woodblock print of* c. *1875 shows the full splendour of the King's Library, 'one of the finest rooms in London'.*

of the beam'. The beams were linked by wrought iron fireplates. The central section is a cast iron arch with girders supporting the beam ends. The bookcases are of oak, the floors oak inlaid with mahogany. The four pillars in the centre are of polished Aberdeen granite with capitals of Derbyshire alabaster. There should have been twelve but, not for the first or last time, the Trustees had insufficient funds since, although the rough columns cost a modest £60, polishing brought the bill up to over £1,000. Smirke was therefore obliged to turn eight into pilasters. The projections of the walls are of scagliola 'marble'.

The King's Library was thrown open for inspection in October 1831 and closed almost immediately since it was not intended for the edification of the general public. A few privileged people only were permitted to see it by ticket. For four months at the time of the Great Exhibition in 1851 some of the library rooms were opened as part of a circular tour of closed areas of the Museum. The Trustees were concerned about dust and dirt brought in by the masses and it did not become a public thoroughfare until 1857.

From the mid-nineteenth century the King's Library was used for exhibitions. The bookpresses are original, although the protective brass trellis was removed when they were altered as part of a phased project starting in 1852 to glaze all bookcases in this area. The ceiling was reinforced in 1995 to ensure that it fully meets modern floor loading requirements.

To the south of the King's Library was the Manuscripts Saloon, later used as a workroom by the staff. This was described in the *Illustrated London News* of 1851 as 'a large and heavy-looking room, whose dingy walls and blackened ceiling – strangers to whitewash for three-and-twenty years – give it a solemn, grim, literary look.'

The Manuscripts Saloon became an exhibition gallery in 1857, the Keeper of Manuscripts insisting on a partition to protect his staff from public gaze. Brass door frames glazed with plate glass had by then replaced the brass trellis doors of the bookcases. The ceiling (the floor of the 'Asiatic Saloon' above) was reinforced with additional, now visible, beams in 1933. A staff study at the south-eastern corner in 1938 became the 'Bible Room', used for temporary library exhibitions, and was in 1977 renamed the 'Crawford Room' after the 26th, 27th and 28th Earls of Crawford (all Museum Trustees).

Further south still were what came to be called the 'Middle' and 'South' rooms, completed in 1827. In 1829 these, with places for 120 readers, replaced the old overcrowded reading room in Montagu House. When the 1838 Reading Room opened (p. 24) they were allocated solely for the use of the Department of Manuscripts.

A mezzanine floor was inserted in the South Room in the 1970s to increase manuscript storage capacity.

The long gallery immediately above the King's Library, completed in 1831, was originally intended for the national collection of oil paintings, but with the establishment of the National Gallery in 1824 the space was appropriated to natural history. In the mid-nineteenth century it presented a splendidly cluttered sight, the walls decked with the remains of the Trustees' paintings and (in pre-conservation days) the collection of horns of deer and rhinoceri. In the wall cases were masses of stuffed birds, 'raptorial', 'nocturnal raptorial', 'perching', 'wide-gaped perching' and so on. Table cases contained birds' eggs and 'shells of molluscous animals'. After the departure of natural history in the 1880s (p. 52), a very cluttered ethnographical display moved in.

In its southern extremity, from 1828, was located the Print Room removed from Montagu House. This moved to the north-west corner of the building in 1842 (pp. 26-8).

The Tutankhamun exhibition in 1972 displaced Ethnography. The gallery now mainly houses Romano-British and Celtic collections. The rooms at the southern end were allocated as studies to British and Medieval Antiquities and Ethnography in the 1880s and now include exhibition galleries.

In 1845 it was decided to build a long, low gallery on the east of the King's Library and the Department of Manuscripts in order to provide further book storage. Perforated iron bookstacks, the precursors of the more famous ones to be constructed around the Round Reading Room (pp. 48-50), were designed by the then Keeper of Printed Books, Antonio Panizzi. This wing was completed in about 1850.

This addition was much altered by the British Library in the 1980s with the introduction of additional offices and windows. The southern section of the 'iron library' known as the 'Old Sanskrit Library' survives, as does the Keeper of Printed Books' office, first occupied by Antonio Panizzi in 1856. The furnishings include the future Principal Librarian's mahogany-cased lavatory and a concealed trap door, perhaps for a speedy escape.

11. *The Eastern Zoological Gallery, photographed in 1875 by Frederick York, was at that time little altered since the collections were installed in 1838. Most of the paintings, arranged by John Edward Gray, Keeper of Zoology, were transferred to the National Portrait Gallery in 1877. The Smirke interior has recently been restored, and the southern end is now the Weston Gallery of Roman Britain.*

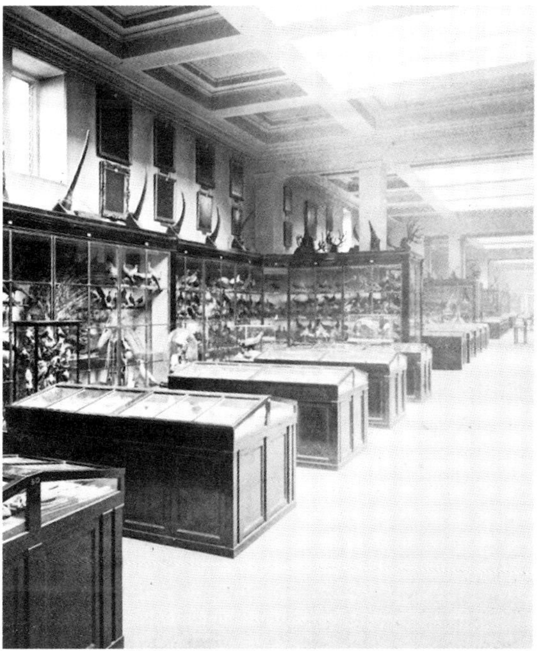

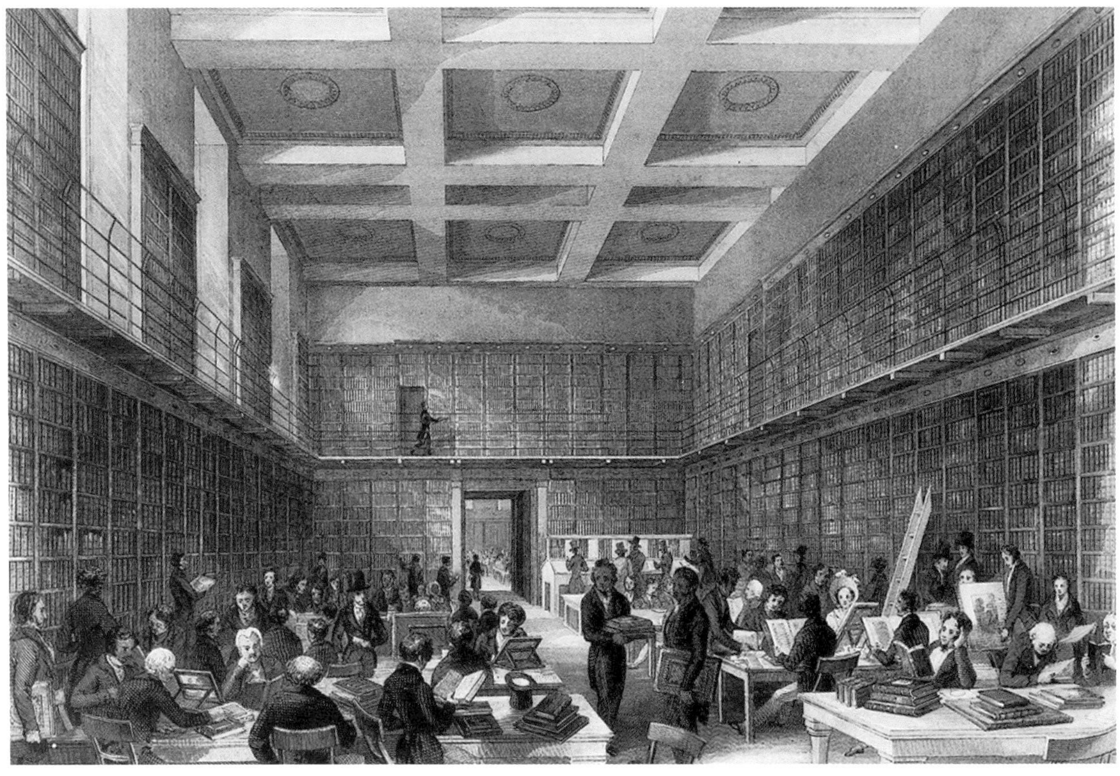

12. *The 1838 Reading Room, from* London Interiors, *1841: '. . . two spacious, lofty rooms which, not withstanding the party wall, may be described as one hall, contracted in the middle, and bulging out at both ends like a square hour glass, or a dandy, when dandies existed and wore stays . . .' (Knight's* London, *1844).*

THE NORTH WING

Plans for the North Wing were approved in principle by the Trustees on 11 July 1823. Smirke produced a more detailed design in March 1833. Ground was broken for the foundation of the new building on 10 September 1833 and the first bricks were laid on 17 October 1833.

The North Wing was opened in January 1838. As in Smirke's other wings, there were three main levels: basements, 'ground' and upper. The ground floor and basements were given over almost entirely to the Department of Printed Books, with storage for 280,000 volumes. Since, unfortunately, the library already had 230,000 volumes at the time of the move, this did little to solve long-term problems, for the space was expected to be filled within four or five years. The upper galleries were for the display of mineralogy and geology.

The 1838 Reading Room

The North Wing included a reading room (actually two rooms), which opened on 8 September 1838. This was the sixth, and much improved, location since readers were first admitted in 1759. Karl Marx initially worked here, as did Charles Dickens, Dante Gabriel Rossetti, Richard Cobden and George Meredith. The rooms were lofty and capacious, although there was criticism from those who actually had to work there, since the windows were too high and in one room only on one side. *The Times* indeed commented that 'rooms of such large dimensions are almost too spacious for quiet study and repose'. There were originally 168 places, which were in due course increased to 208 to cope with demand. Entry was through spiked iron gates along a lane between recently built houses on the south side of Montague Place.

The 1838 Reading Room, vacated on completion of the Round Reading Room in 1857 (pp. 47-8), was much altered in the 1930s by the insertion of a mezzanine and new windows (pp. 63-4). The lower part is now the Mexican Gallery and the Chase Manhattan Gallery of North America.

The Great or Large Room

Glimpsed from the Reading Room was the 'Large Room'. This jutted out into the half-moon space to the north of the Trustees' property which formed part of the original grant of land. It was used for book storage, the public not being admitted, and was described in 1851 as 'a saloon of colossal dimensions though much broken up by the recesses on each side, the projections forming which are terminated by square pillars supporting the roof. It measures 80 ft long and 90 ft wide [24.4 x 27.4 m], and occupies the whole depth of the north front, so that it is lighted with windows on both sides . . . .'

The Large Room was extended as part of the Burnet scheme of 1906-14 (p. 62). This in turn was much altered between the wars (pp. 63-4); only the shell of the inter-war room remains.

Parallel to the larger rooms on the ground floor was a series of rooms used for book storage and library offices. On the east a lobby led into the 'Banksian Room' which, until the 1960s, con-

13. *The Large Room, opened to the public during the Great Exhibition (*Illustrated London News, *7 June 1851).*

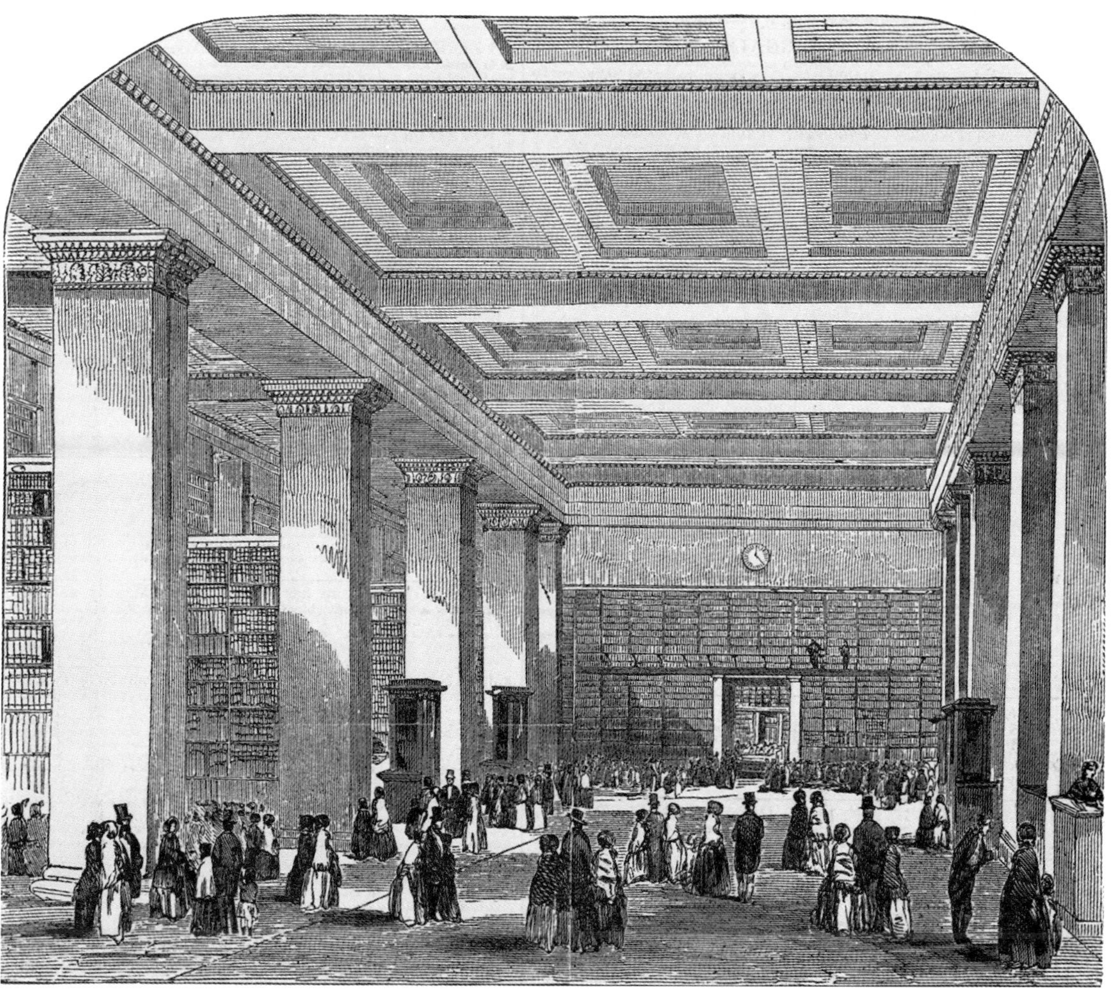

tained the library of Sir Joseph Banks (1744-1820), Captain James Cook's patron and, as President of the Royal Society, a Trustee of the Museum from 1778. When the public were briefly admitted in June 1851 they saw 'some book shelves fixed against the elsewhere blank walls of the vestibule, with a corkscrew staircase of dizzy height leading up to them'; then followed 'a room of moderate size, but giving, like the succeeding rooms, with one exception, an impression of unnecessary darkness as well as of loss of space above the gallery book-cases.' To the west, matching the Banksian Rooms, was the Cracherode Room, where the library bequeathed by Clayton Mordaunt Cracherode (1730-99) was housed from 1843. (Cracherode also gave a superlative collection of prints and drawings, engraved gems and coins.) It was here that the news that a member of staff had shot himself is said to have been greeted by his superior with the comment, 'Did he damage the [book] bindings?'. Adjacent to this was the 'Egyptian Vestibule'.

These rooms and the labyrinthine offices above are now largely reconstructions following the insertion of mezzanine floors in the 1930s (pp. 63-4).

The Arched Room

At the far west end of the North Wing is the lofty Arched Room with its great west window, a later addition to Smirke's quadrangular scheme, which gives an impression of what the other rooms in this wing must have been like. The first plans were put forward in 1837. Two storeys only were planned, but in 1839 it was decided to build the room to the same height as the other rooms in the wing. The foundations were laid in May 1839 and it was completed in 1841.

The Arched Room is today largely unchanged except that some of the bookpresses have been glazed. From the turn of the century it contained (amongst other material) the library's collection of incunabula and also until recent years the infamous 'private case' where books not deemed suitable for the general reader were locked away.

Recent remodelling of the upper galleries of the North Wing revealed that they were originally planned with side, rather than central, doors. In January 1842, at the request of Sir Robert Smirke, James Braidwood, Superintendent of the London Fire Brigade, visited the new building to check 'the probabilities of fires taking place and to extending the means of preventing them.' His report pinpointed the potential weak spots, and Smirke was soon arranging for the construction of additional fire walls, built to the height of the roof, and the resiting of strengthened door frames. Changes in this range of galleries were probably part of this programme.

These rooms were usually on the route for tours by distinguished visitors and amused some, but not all. During a visit by the King of Prussia in February 1842 the royal party included this suite in their visit and it was reported that:

> Mr Konig waited at the entrance of the Geological Room, and explained the History of some of the Saurian Remains, the skeleton from Guadeloupe, the Tortoise from Hydrabad, the Meteoric collection etc. Mr Gray was unable to arrest much of His Majesty's attention to the Zoology after he had looked at the Painting of the Dodo.

Natural history was replaced by antiquities in the 1880s. There were originally windows on the north, east and west sides, but these were largely blocked in at an early stage to provide more wall space for exhibition, and skylights were enlarged in 1912. The parallel galleries originally had skylights but now have glazed barrel roofs, introduced in 1934.

The Print and Insect Rooms

Also completed in 1840-41 and extending south from the Arched Room on the same line as the Elgin Room (p. 34), but not joined to it, were the Print and Insect Rooms. In 1863 the *Builder* published a description of the former, now lost, room which lay off the north stairs.

> [The entrance] is in no way marked . . . The initiated . . . pull a bell, and speedily the door is

14. *The Arched Room (from* London Interiors, *1841): ' . . . the Double galleries of this handsome apartment produce an impression of additional height, while their pierced iron floors and the arching of the piers of the recesses give the room an appearance of lightness and elegance' (*Illustrated London News, *1851).*

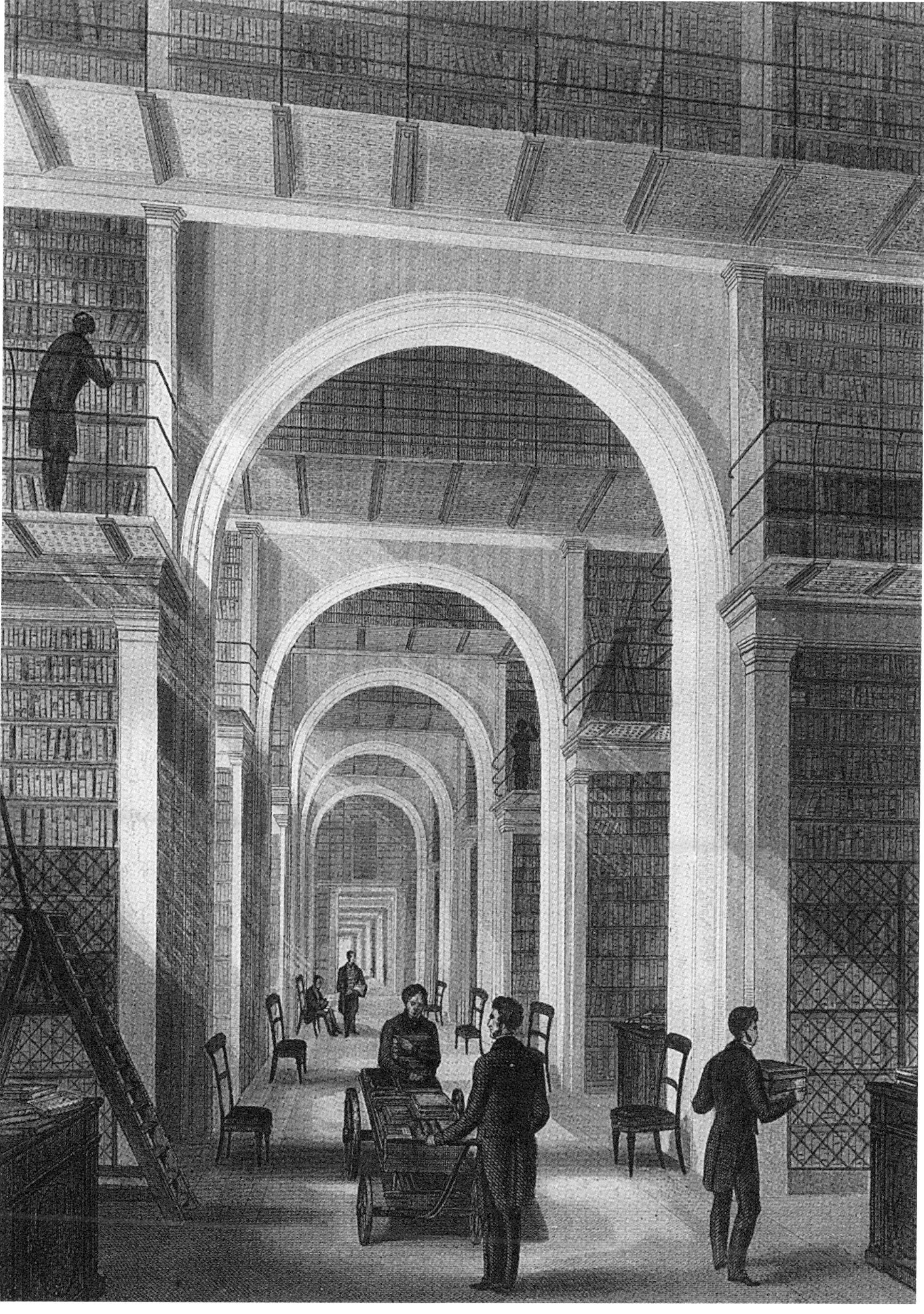

> opened, and admission is given to a long passage, lined with cases in which there are large volumes containing prints and drawings. Beyond is the Print-room, a large, well-lighted and handsome apartment. In the central space there are tables and seats for the use of visitors. Handsome cases are fixed around, which are occupied by large and richly bound volumes. On the top of the cases are capital busts of poets, painters, architects, engravers, and distinguished royal and other patrons of art.

Below the Print Room was the Insect Room, where the greater part of the Museum's collection was housed in cabinets, available only by appointment.

The Print and Insect Rooms no longer exist, having been reconstructed in 1885 to provide space for classical antiquities. The area now comprises the Payava and Caryatid Rooms.

THE DEMOLITION OF MONTAGU HOUSE

The demolition of the north part of Montagu House was sanctioned in March 1842. On 22 July 1842 Robert Smirke reported that:

> ... the Materials of the Building which formed the northern half of the old Mansion are now cleared away and the workmen are excavating the ground for the foundations of the new Building, and if the weather during the latter part of the year should be favorable I have reason to hope the walls of the whole south side of the Quadrangle will be raised to receive the roofs before Christmas.

Before the end of autumn 1843 the narrow galleries leading to the Townley Gallery and the western portion of what remained of Montagu House were removed. The rest of it disappeared in the course of 1845, although the gatehouse and wall went later, in 1850.

An ineffectual attempt was made in 1839 by Heathcote Russell to save the renowned painted walls and ceilings. On 28 March 1842 a Mr Seguier reported that the paintings had been executed directly upon the plaster and would be impossible to preserve. In October 1842 Russell resubmitted his proposal and in February 1845 he offered to remove the paintings at his own expense. Although he was shown the site by the Clerk of Works, there are no further references to the proposals in the Trustees' papers. Since the Trustees had looked favourably upon Mr Russell, it is possible that at least some of the paintings were removed, particularly since Russell appeared to be interested in removing representative sections. If this is so, their whereabouts remain a mystery. There is a Museum story that some shady but profitable deal was made by William Scivier, the porter, who agreed to take the frescoes off the Trustees' hands and sold them to persons unknown.

Unfashionable Montagu House, once one of the finest buildings in London, was gone, and it is said that few mourned its passing, apart from the essayist Charles Lamb, who regretted the loss of 'the princely apartments of poor condemned Montagu House' in which he had frequently dined out with the staff, as had Coleridge, Southey

15. *A poster of 20 April 1843 advertising the sale of building materials from the western section of Montagu House, recently demolished 'by order of the Commissioners of Her Majesty's Woods, Forests, Land Revenues, Works and Buildings'.*

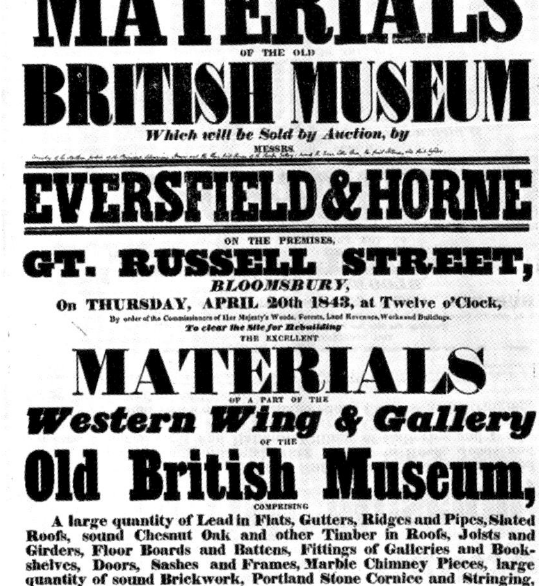

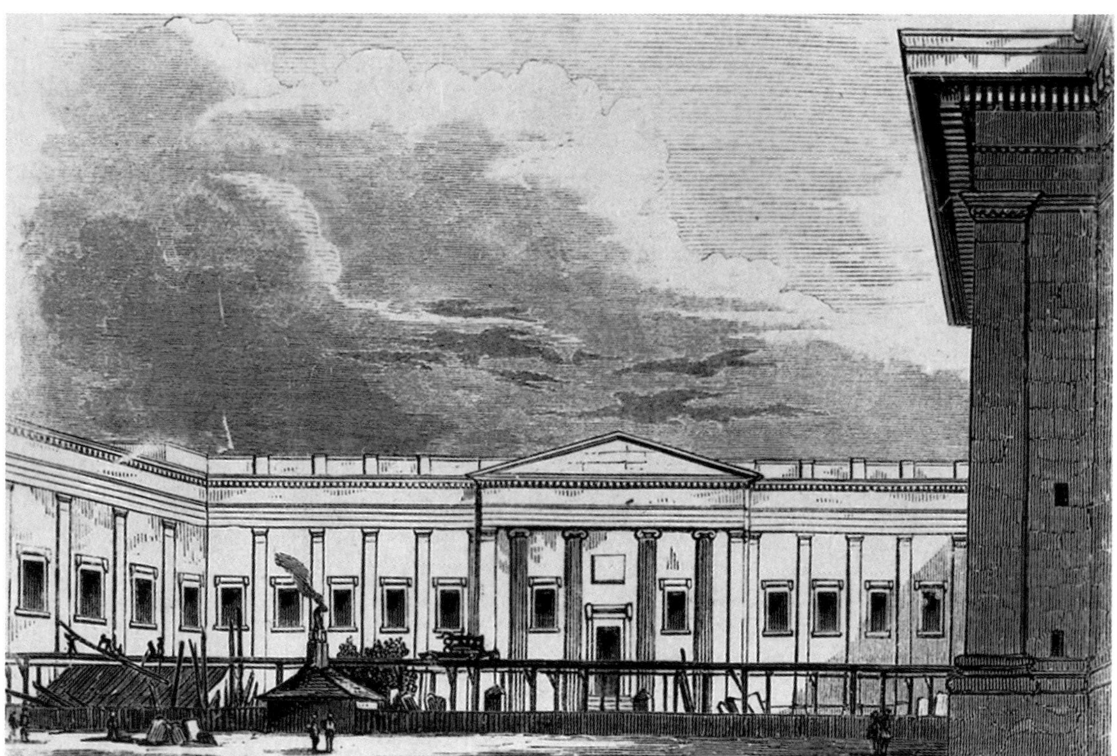

16. *The Inner Courtyard during the construction of the South Wing* c. *1845, '. . . presented an unoccupied space, which Mr Grenville said, when he first saw it "would make the finest stonemason's yard in Europe". It had . . . been laid out as a grass plot with a broad gravel walk down the centre. The grass, however, never looked very green, as the surrounding buildings excluded the necessary light and sun . . . a dull miserable looking place' (Cowtan, 1872).*

and Wordsworth. There is a description of the decaying building around 1835, a few years before its demise: 'As viewed from the spot where I am now standing, it has little in appearance to recommend it. Neither its guarded gateways, its square turrets, its front of dirty red brick, nor its old crazy cupola, is of an alluring character . . .' (*Old Humphrey's Walks in London*, Religious Tract Society, published 1843 but referring to the 1830s).

THE SOUTH WING

With the gradual disappearance of Montagu House, work began on the northern side of the new South Wing in July 1842, plans for the principal floor and basements having been approved in June. In 1843 the south-west portion (the Secretary's offices and boardroom) began to rise. The south front and colonnade were practically finished in 1846.

The great colonnade

To the general public, at least, Smirke's elevations for the south front of the Museum were bound to come as a surprise. A quarter of a century had passed since Smirke is thought to have produced his initial design, and minimal attention had been given to it. Architectural fashions had moved on, and the *Builder*, never averse to criticism, especially when directed towards the Museum, commented: '. . . to what are we to ascribe the universal apathy manifested on this occasion? Is it that because the British Museum is not in the Gothic style, and does not particularly interest Camdenists, Ecclesiologists and Puginists, it is therefore a matter of perfect indifference what be made of it?'

The *Synopsis* summed up the south front as follows:

> . . . the entrance portico [is] eight columns in width, and two intercolumniations in projection. On either side is an advancing wing, giving to the entire front an extent of three hundred and seventy feet [112.7 m]; the whole surrounded by a colonnade of forty-four columns, raised upon a stylobate five feet and a half high [1.7 m]. The columns are five feet [1.5 m] at their lower diameter, and forty-five feet [13.7 m] high; the height from the pavement of the front courtyard to the top of the entablature of the colonnade, sixty-six feet and a half [20.3 m].

The columns are a classical composite, adapted from the capitals of the temple of Athena Polias at Priene, and the bases of the temple of Dionysos at Teos. The colonnade and facings are Portland stone.

On seeing a drawing in 1843 the *Builder* thundered:

> Sir Robert Smirke's conduct in this business leaves him with scarcely one to defend him . . . The public, if we are to judge from what is said by all its organs, by every authority on matters of art, have well-nigh lost all patience, and are abandoning themselves to the extreme of chagrin and disappointment . . . The thing is wanting in dignity, in character, in every thing except the most effete and out wrought mannerism; a portico and pediment as the end of something stuck at the side of something, and the whole hemmed in as if two neighbour proprietors had taken possession or broken a compact that had enjoined an undisturbed ground vacancy upon which Sir Robert had relied for setting off his building. Then there is the neat range of booking-office or counting-house windows, dignified by a screen facade of columns.
>
> Oh, such botching and patching! We have no words for it.

Whatever its architectural merits and demerits, in time the colonnade became familiar and accepted. Because of the buildings jostling round it, it has never really been seen from a distance, to full advantage, but it is a powerful sight, suddenly looming like a dinosaur out of the shops and cafés of Bloomsbury. By the time Smirke's *DNB* entry was written (1897) the façade could be described as 'the most imposing in the metropolis'.

The public were not allowed on the colonnade until the 1930s, when seats were provided and for a time bay trees were placed in tubs between the columns.

The Front Hall

The Museum never closed to visitors during the rebuilding period. A temporary entrance was constructed with ramps on the western side of the colonnade and used until the Front Hall opened to the public on 19 April 1847.

As in Montagu House, the grand staircase is on the left, although as late as 1841 the Trustees were still pondering which side would be best. The style of the columns is Grecian Doric and the floor is of York stone. The balustrade of the staircase and the carved ornamental vases are of Huddlestone stone. Massive plinths intended as sculpture pedestals (p. 42) were made of grey Aberdeen granite, and the walls on either side of the central flight were cased with red Aberdeen granite. Although it was part of Robert Smirke's scheme, he was absent through illness from 1845 and formally resigned in 1846. The work was therefore taken over by Sydney Smirke, who is credited with the decision to redecorate in the elaborate polychromatic scheme executed by Messrs Collman & Davis in 1847 (col. pl. 5).

It has been argued that this scheme would not have been favoured by Robert, but in the years since the building began in 1823 tastes had changed and Robert is not known to have voiced any disagreement. Sydney Smirke set out his opinions in a report to the Trustees in December 1846 asking for their permission to go ahead with the decoration. He wrote:

> If done sparingly and cautiously; in strict conformity with ancient examples, and confined chiefly to the mouldings, I am quite confident of a satisfactory result. Whatever doubt there may be as to the propriety of this kind of embellishment in the exhibition rooms, I apprehend there would be none as to its introduction in the hall and Staircase where there is more architectural effect than in any other part of the interior of the building.

The *Builder* was well disposed towards the 'modern' colour scheme in the Front Hall:

> . . . the polychrome enrichments have been applied with very considerable success. The sunk

> panels are blue, with a yellow star in each; the enrichments are variously coloured, red and white predominating, and the stiles, beams, etc., are covered with frets, guilloche, and scrolls, in flat colours, for all of which precedents were sought in the Museum collection.

The Front Hall has reverted to its original size with the demolition of the 1877 extension (p. 51) to make way for the Great Court. The plinths on either side of the staircase were removed in 1964 but have since been restored.

The Grenville Library, Egerton and Map Rooms

To the west of the Front Hall is the Grenville Library, which dates from the same period. Sir Thomas Grenville, MP (1755-1846), an eminent bibliophile, Trustee and friend of Panizzi, left a bequest of 16,000 works in 20,240 volumes. Despite opposition from the Keeper of Manuscripts to whom the space had been promised and who immediately began to cram the shelves with manuscripts, the Grenville collection was moved into this area and the room took Grenville's name.

Parallel to the Grenville Library the first high-ceilinged room off the Front Hall to the right was initially the waiting room for the Department of Manuscripts, and beyond this were the Map Room and South Manuscripts Room. In the 1880s the waiting room was renamed the Egerton Room after Francis Henry Egerton, 8th Earl of Bridgewater (d. 1829), who bequeathed a collection of sixty-seven volumes of manuscripts plus £5,000, the income of which was to be used for purchases.

The public were not admitted to the Grenville Library until 1857, after which the room for many years housed an exhibition of manuscripts. The Egerton and Map Rooms were much altered by the inclusion of a mezzanine for manuscript storage, completed in 1970.

The Roman Gallery

To the left of the entrance was the Roman Gallery, where the visitor had to pass a forbidding gauntlet of statues and busts and, for a time, British antiquities. The *Building News* criticized it as 'narrow, gloomy and not in accordance with the grand Ionic portico'. Nathaniel Hawthorne described it in 1870:

> We went first among some antique marbles, – busts, statues, terminal gods, with several of the Roman emperors among them. We saw here the bust whence Haydon took his ugly and ridiculous likeness of Nero, – a foolish thing to do. Julius Caesar was there, too, looking more like a modern old man than any other bust in the series ....

This room became a bookshop in the 1960s.

The south-west corner

An imposing Boardroom with oak panelled walls, green marble fireplaces and an elaborate ceiling was constructed for the Trustees and completed in 1849. Here, for many years, they held their regular Saturday meetings, and in more recent times, until financial restraints bit, objects from all over the world would jostle for space on shelves and tables awaiting purchase like some vast sale of work. A long corridor led past the Boardroom to the oak panelled room with the Readers' Admissions desk, where for decades potential readers were required

17. *The Trustees' Boardroom c. 1965, presided over by a portrait of Sir Hans Sloane: some proposed acquisitions are displayed for consideration. The Trustees' ceremonial mace can be seen on the table.*

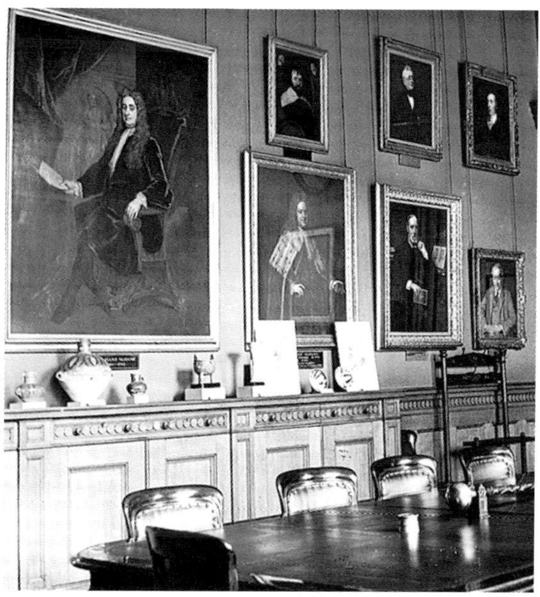

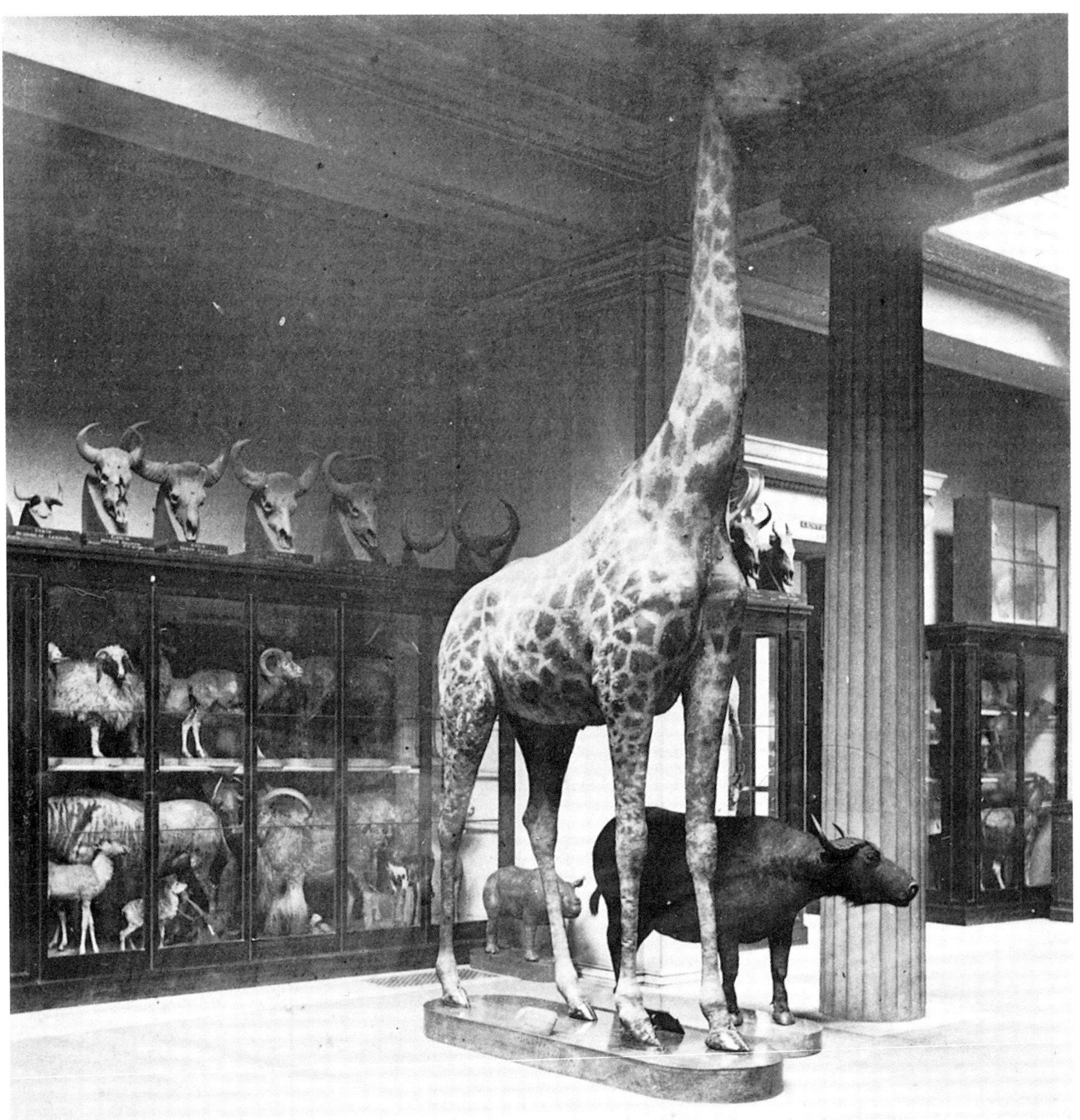

18. *The Central Saloon in 1875, two years before Sir John Taylor's extension to the north. The giraffe captured here, and another out of shot, were from the trio originally stationed at the top of the staircase in Montagu House. The third did not survive.*

to convince an often supercilious Admissions Clerk of their bona fides and sign a register indicating that they were over twenty-one and prepared to abide by the Library's rules. An enlargement of the linking corridor to the Residences (p. 40) constituted the Principal Librarian's Office, hazardously reached by means of an unexpected step.

Above were the Medal Room, the Gold Ornament Room and studies (now the offices of the Department of Greek and Roman Antiquities). The most westerly gallery, now the HSBC Money

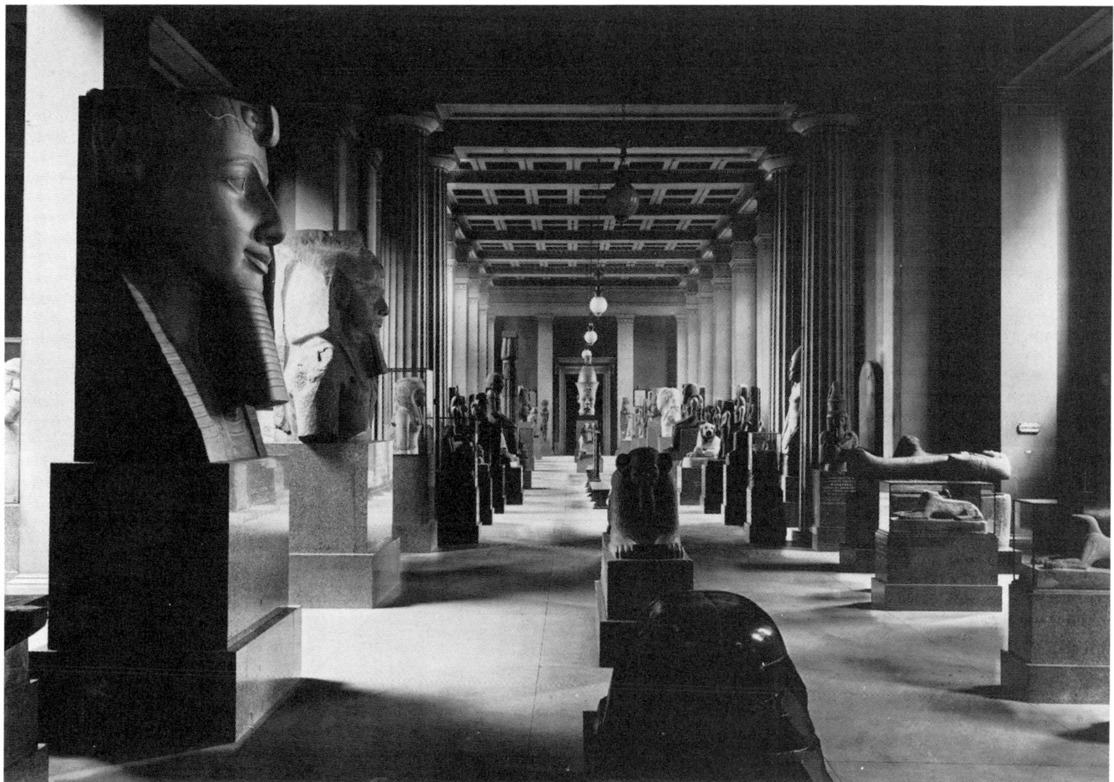

Gallery, housed such of the Ethnography collection as was on display in the mid-nineteenth century. The central saloon at the top of the main stairs originally held 'Mammalia' (including the famous stuffed giraffes), which were succeeded after the departure of natural history to South Kensington in the 1880s (p. 52) by prehistory and, in the 1960s, the Hinton St Mary Mosaic (now removed). In the other galleries at this level natural history gave way to British and Medieval Antiquities. From one of these rooms the so-called 'Botanical Staircase' (a name still retained) ran the length of the building.

The medals transferred to a new room in 1892 (p. 57). The Gold Ornament Room was not restored after the Second World War because such objects were no longer exhibited out of context. This south-westerly corner was much altered by the construction of the New Wing (pp. 68-9), including the flooring-over of a gallery above Readers' Admissions to construct what is now the Pamela Hartwell Room, much used for Museum entertaining. In the central saloon at the top of the great staircase a wall with two entrances and a niche was destroyed during the Second World War and not rebuilt.

19. *The Egyptian Sculpture Gallery looking north, c. 1890, soon after the installation of electric light.*

THE WEST WING

Egyptian Sculpture Gallery

The northern section of the West Wing, including the 'central saloon', was one of the earliest parts of the building to be completed. The diarist Thomas Conrath recorded on 11 February 1826 that workmen had begun removing the terrace on the west side of the garden for the foundation of 'a new building for the sculptures' and the first bricks were laid later that month. It was finished in the autumn of 1831, while the southern section had to await the demolition of the Townley Gallery.

The northern part of the gallery housed Egyptian antiquities (including those transferred from the Townley Gallery), installed by summer 1834, and in the central area were initially classical antiquities. The Townley Gallery was taken down in 1846 and the southern half of the western gallery then built. The classical sculptures were in due course transferred elsewhere and the whole taken over by Egyptian material in February 1854. Nathaniel Hawthorne, who was not over-keen on the Museum, described this room in 1870:

> We passed . . . through Assyrian saloons and Egyptian saloons, – all full of monstrosities and horrible uglinesses, especially the Egyptian . . . Their gigantic statues are certainly very curious. I saw a hand and arm up to the shoulder fifteen feet in length, and made of some stone that seemed harder and heavier than granite, not having lost its polish in all the rough usage that it has undergone . . . Hideous, blubber-lipped faces of giants, and human shapes, with beasts' heads on them.

Smirke's design remained relatively unaltered for over a century. In the mid-1930s the Egyptian sculptures were rearranged in chronological sequence, beginning at the northern end. A further rearrangement, to a design by Robin Wade and Associates, was carried out, opening in 1981, with the chronological order now from south to north. Two small side galleries were then constructed on the east, but these have been removed to make space for the Great Court.

The rooms above the Egyptian Sculpture Gallery were also completed in two phases. The most southerly gallery housed the nascent British collection from 1852. Beyond were classical and then Egyptian antiquities (mummies), the latter room described as 'a large and handsomely finished saloon, lighted from the roof'. In the reallocation of space following the departure of natural history in the 1880s, Greek and Roman antiquities took over the entire space.

The roofs were destroyed in 1941 and temporarily replaced. In the 1980s the Smirke design was largely restored and the floors strengthened.

Elgin, Phigaleia and insects

Few people have been able to trace the architectural history of the western galleries and it is not something that can easily be described intelligibly, since changes in nomenclature can trip the unwary. Thus the First Elgin Room becomes the Second Elgin Room and then the Nereid Room; the second First Elgin Room then turns for a short while into the Mausoleum Room prior to the construction of the Mausoleum Room proper; the Phigaleian Room suddenly fills with Roman sculpture and the Phigaleian sculptures re-emerge where insects once held sway.

The first room to be constructed beyond Smirke's West Wing was the Elgin Room, since a substantial and permanent location for the Parthenon sculptures, still in their temporary abode, was long overdue. Robert Smirke's original plan for this addition, drawn in 1826, called for a gallery projecting from the West Wing westwards. This was soon revised beyond recognition following the intervention of the Trustees and their artistic adviser, Richard Westmacott. By 1830 a proposed upper floor to the room had been abandoned, resulting in the introduction of natural overhead lighting for the sculptures. Also, the room would now run parallel to the West Wing. The revisions were approved, and by November 1831 the Parthenon sculptures had found a more 'permanent' home, which opened to the public in July 1832. The connection to the West Wing was at first by a temporary corridor. This was enlarged to take the Phigaleian marbles.

In 1850 an additional Elgin Gallery was proposed. This was built on to the southern end of the Elgin Room and was ready to receive sculptures by the summer of 1852. In 1868 another, additional, Elgin Room was completed to the north of the original Elgin Room and connected with what had been the Print Room (pp. 26-8) in the North Wing. This is the basic structure of these galleries. Readers wishing to follow the tortuous progression of Elgin, Phigaleia, insects and other sculptures from this point may like to consult Jenkins (1992).

The Parthenon sculptures ('Elgin marbles') are now in the Duveen Gallery (pp. 64-5). The greater part of the old Elgin Gallery is taken up by the Nereid monument with, to the north, the Payava tomb and Caryatid from the Erechtheion and, to the south, the Phigaleian marbles (now known as the Bassae frieze) in a mezzanine; beyond them are the Harpy tomb and other objects. These galleries were much altered in the 1960s. The original Phigaleian Room is now occupied by Roman sculpture.

The Lycian Gallery

The Lycian Gallery was constructed as a westwards extension of the Townley Gallery, initially to house sculptures excavated in Lycia (Anatolia) by Charles Fellows, particularly the remains of monumental tombs. Plans were submitted in March 1844 and work on site began in April. The Lycian gallery was opened to the public in December 1847.

Later known as the 'Archaic Room', the Lycian Gallery, now housing objects from Archaic Greece, was altered in the 1980s by the insertion of a mezzanine for the Department of Coins and Medals. There was originally a door in the east wall leading to the Assyrian Transept.

Graeco-Roman Rooms

A room parallel and to the south of the Lycian Gallery was completed in 1854 (opened 1855) with a staircase at the west end leading down to a basement where there were 'miscellaneous sculptures of subordinate rank'. A small anteroom was formed between the new building and the south-west corner of the main Museum. In the smaller room were displayed 'representations of human personages' and in the larger 'divine or heroic' personages.

These rooms, now containing Cycladic and Greek Bronze Age material were much altered in the 1960s redesign. The public restaurant of the New Wing (p. 69) was attached to the west end; the old basement closed.

SIR ROBERT SMIRKE AND HIS TEAM

Of Sir Robert Smirke the *DNB* remarks that 'the great majority of his works, both public and private, were classical, massive in construction, heavy and sombre in treatment', an apt description for the British Museum. At the beginning of his career he was articled briefly to Sir John Soane, and in 1799, prophetically, he received the Royal Academy's gold medal for a design for a national museum. From 1801 to 1805 he travelled in Italy,

20. *In this 1845 watercolour by George Scharf the foundations for the Lycian Gallery take shape as the Townley Gallery, on the left, awaits demolition. Behind the Military Guard House the West Residence is nearing completion. The steeple of St George's Church can be seen in the distance.*

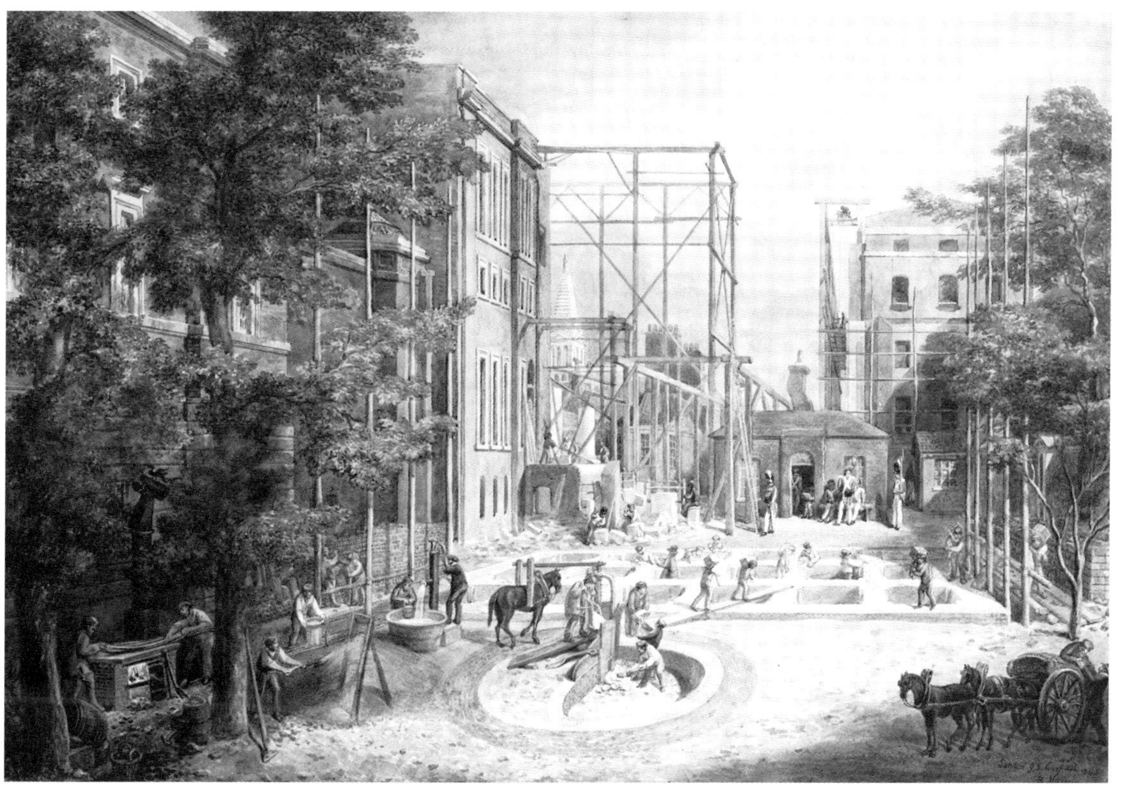

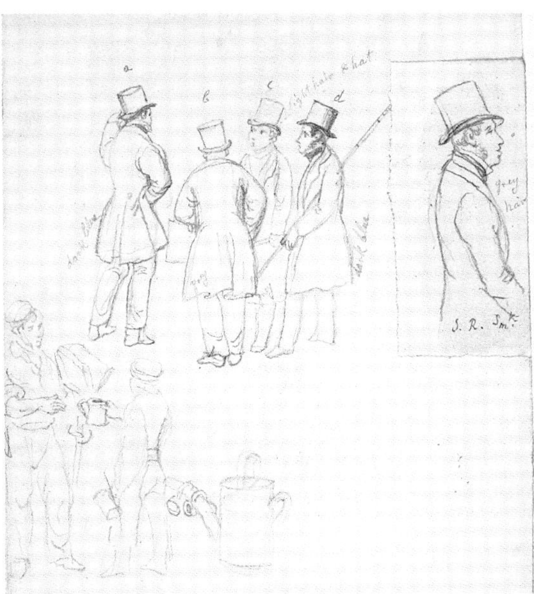

21. *A sketch made by George Scharf in 1844 or 1845 shows the architect and his immediate team: (a) Mr Baker, Builder (related to Smirke by marriage); (b) Mr Denison, Clerk of Works; (c) Mr Farrow, Superintendent of masons; (d) Mr Nichols, [in charge of] Bricklayers. To the right is Sir Robert Smirke, with the artist's annotation 'grey hair and top hat'. Below, a boy hands refreshments to a hod carrier.*

Greece and Sicily, studying architecture and soaking up the classical past. He was appointed architect to the Board of Trade in 1807 and was responsible for the greater portion of the Mint on Tower Hill (1809-11). In 1815 he became one of the three official architects to the Board of Works (the others were John Nash and Sir John Soane). Commissions for royal and government buildings were divided among the three. Among Smirke's projects were the extension of Somerset House, the rebuilding of the London Custom House, and the construction of the British Museum and the General Post Office (both begun in 1823). He also had a considerable private practice.

In 1832 the Office of Works was reorganized, becoming the Office of Woods and Works; commissions were thrown open to the profession, and the posts of 'attached architect' abolished. Smirke received a compensatory knighthood and had the pleasure of seeing his commission on architectural projects, now undertaken privately, increase from 3 to 5 per cent. He retained his connection with the British Museum.

Smirke published little and his reports in the Museum archive rarely set out the ideas behind his work. He must have been under immense pressure dealing with the Museum project – uncertainties of funding were linked to the arrival of more and more antiquities, books and natural history specimens which had to go somewhere. He was frequently subject to interference on points of detail from the Trustees and Richard Westmacott. Occasionally his temper almost snaps at yet another ill-thought-out last-minute direction. He was, however, a professional architect/engineer, a good administrator who rationalized estimating, measuring and cost accounting. He is particularly noted for his use of modern and innovative practices and materials. In ill health for a number of years, he was absent from the Museum from 1845 and formally resigned in 1846, having been appointed to the Commission for London Improvement. In 1859 he retired to Cheltenham.

Sydney Smirke

Robert Smirke's younger brother Sydney was involved in the British Museum project from an early stage. In his letter of resignation, addressed to Alexander Milne, First Commissioner of Works, and dated 2 July 1846, Robert wrote

> . . . however I may regret the necessity, I should retire with the great satisfaction of believing that my plans will be completed in the manner I could best desire, if the direction of them were allowed to remain in the hands of my brother Mr Sydney Smirke. He has already given to the works such superintendance for me as appeared to be necessary during my absence, and having assisted me often from the period of their commencement in the year 1823, he is well acquainted with every part of the Buildings and their construction.

In 1816, at the age of eighteen, Sydney Smirke was already working in his brother's office and it was he who was given the responsibility for carrying the plans for the Temporary Elgin Room (p. 19) to the Museum for the Trustees' approval. When he succeeded his brother in 1846 the rebuilding of the Museum had been in progress for twenty-three years, but the massive south front was barely under way and Saunders' Townley Gallery was awaiting demolition the following winter, to be replaced by the southern section of the new West Wing. Sydney would also be responsible for the subsequent decorative schemes throughout the Museum, additional sculpture galleries and the design for the Round Reading Room, and was to be associated with the Museum for fifty years, considerably longer than his elder brother.

Outside the Museum, Sydney Smirke undertook other projects, including the design of a number of private houses, the reconstruction of the Pantheon in Oxford Street and the restoration of the Savoy Chapel.

The workers

Little is ever said about the vast armies of craftsmen and labourers who built the Museum. The volume of material with which they worked was stupendous: the colonnade alone is said to have been formed of 800 blocks of Portland stone, each 5-9 tons in weight. George Scharf the Elder (1788-1860), who made a vast number of sketches and watercolours, many carefully annotated, of a changing London and its citizens, left one of the few records of these men. We see them with their peaked caps and short jackets: the skilled masons with their mauls, chisels and spirit levels carving the columns (frontispiece); blacksmiths with a set of bellows at a forge 'turning hoop iron for binding the brick walls'; labourers pulling a cart in which is a dressed stone; horses and carts – the only method for conveying the tons of stone to the site. Perched rather precariously at the top of the scaffolding, a pair of men operate a 'traveller' which transports blocks of stone (seen in fig. 16).

There were accidents, and a benevolent fund was set up for the families of those workmen who were injured. Given the scale of the project there were almost certainly fatalities, but none was reported to the Trustees. A Scharf sketch dated 13 August 1847 indicates the risks. It shows a rope breaking while hoisting a 5-ton girder during the building of the Lycian Room and is annotated by the artist, 'It takes 4 hours to wind up a girder. This was 5 tons weight and fell when it was near the top, it broke into 4 pieces nearly breaking a man's leg.'

22. *A drawing by George Scharf of workmen at the forge preparing hoop iron wall ties for the brickwork to the Lycian Room, then under construction, c. 1844.*

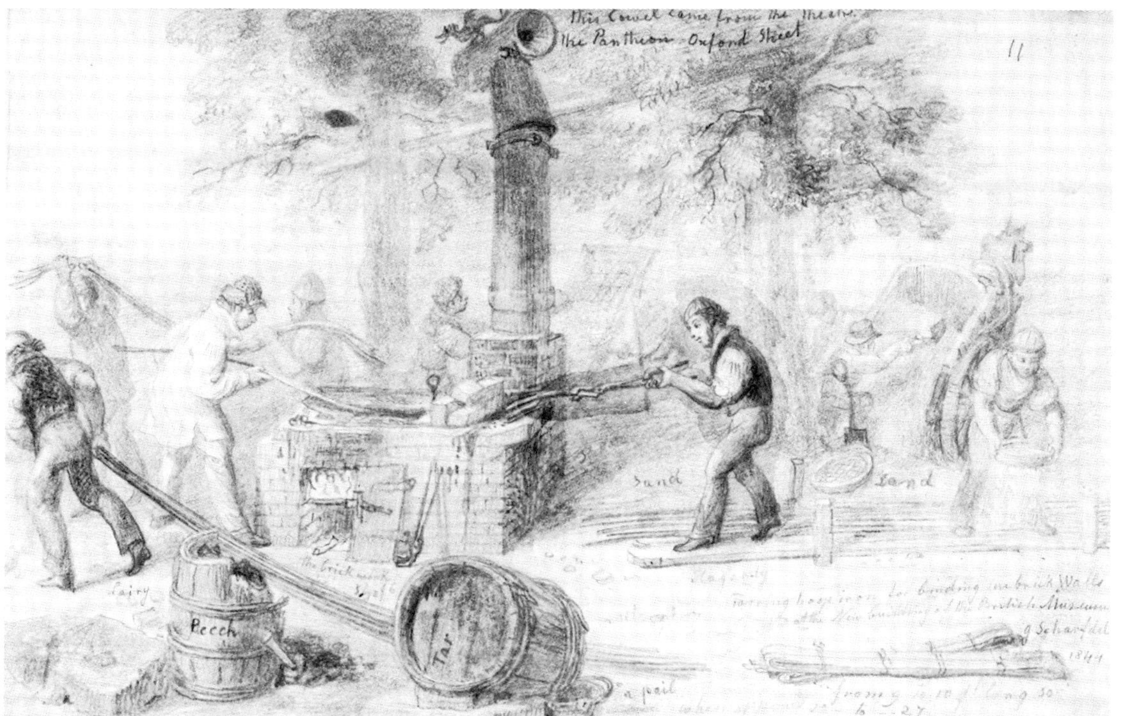

LIFE ON A BUILDING SITE

Life for the senior staff of the Museum, who at that time were obliged to live on the premises, was not easy and the Scharf drawings conjure up the noise and dust. Sir Frederic Madden (Keeper of Manuscripts) memorialized the Trustees in July 1847 concerning

> . . . the extreme annoyances, privations and discomforts, which he and his family have suffered for four years in being obliged to reside in a portion of the old Museum building still standing, during which time the masons' work for hewing stones was carried on close beneath his windows and not only the insufferable dirt and noise consequent thereon but the indecencies of the work people and strangers in front of his residence, constantly to be endured.

He continues:

> Sir F Madden has not received from Sir Robert Smirke or the Contractor for the works the common civility one man expects from another and Sir Henry Ellis's house was about to be pulled down without any notice whilst Lady Madden was in an ill state of health, and daily expecting her confinement. In fact, it was owing entirely to the good natured interference of the Porter at the gate, that the pulling down was delayed until Lady M and her children were removed into the country . . . The supply of excellent water behind his residence was cut off in making the west wing of the new building and he is now indebted for a daily supply to his fishmonger. For a long time after Sir H Ellis's house was pulled down, a host of rats infested Sir F M's apartments both below and above, and nothing was secure from their depredations, not even linen. At various times one of the attics has swarmed with bugs bred in the old delapidated walls of the building and only to be kept out by repeated whitewashing. And last, but not least, the insecure state of the house itself is such – the western wall being several feet out of

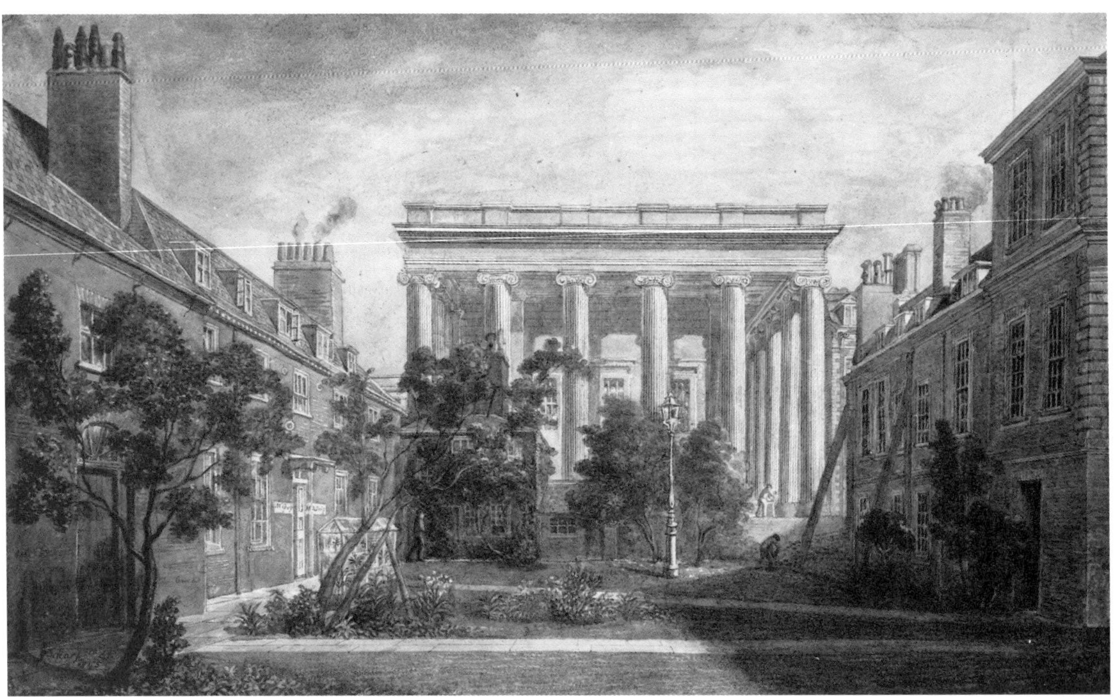

23. *In this watercolour sketch of 1845 by George Scharf the western colonnade of Robert Smirke's building towers over the doomed red-brick 'officers' apartments'. The wooden props mentioned by Sir Frederic Madden are seen on the right. Yet again the garden is about to be be 'deranged'* *(see p.18)* *and a greenhouse removed.*

> the perpendicular and propped up by stays of wood, that Sir F Madden during the winter lives in continual dread of its falling and burying himself and family in its ruins.

As the Museum building grew larger and more complex its maintenance became more of a problem. Having the builders in 150 years ago was not entirely unlike our own day. A letter of complaint written to Sydney Smirke by the Principal Librarian (Panizzi) in 1856 is not unfamiliar:

> The day before yesterday it was found that the Plumber had left one of the Cisterns in my house leaking, he was sent for; one of his workmen came who was tinkering it off and on all yesterday. He went away last night. This morning the cistern is found leaking more than it did before, but the workman had come very early, had carried off his tools without saying a word to any one, has left the place in confusion, has even taken off the ball from the pipe serving the cistern, and let the water run to waste, and now nobody knows what has become of him.
>
> Now this is not a solitary instance of this conduct. Often it happens that painters, upholsterers, etc do the same. They think they have a vested right in the Museum, and that they can attend to it when they like, and as they like . . . This plumber, whose name I don't even know, is one of the most unruly, if you were to find another in his place it would be a good lesson to him and an example to others . . ..

THE FORECOURT

Robert Smirke's initial design of 1823 did not include details of the forecourt. In 1850 Sydney Smirke submitted various proposals to the Trustees (col. pl. 4). One envisaged a pair of widely separated gateways with a semicircular carriageway curving round the front of the portico, while another provided a central entrance with or without a substantial arch. The Trustees' choice, the present single entrance, was Smirke's preferred option as having 'more architectural dignity' and presenting the building to view from the most favourable point. Further, it was what the public was used to.

Two grassed areas protected by low walls were each surrounded by a pathway of York stone paving. Paths of ribbed granite setts were laid to provide links across the gravel to four of the principal staff entrances. The lawns were originally laid on a thick bed of topsoil covering an excess of builders' rubble.

The initially gas-operated lamps were designed by John Walker of York (d. 1853) but completed by his son William Walker (1828-1919), and were alight by summer 1853. They were later converted to electricity and in the early 1880s the central posts were altered from a single to a triple globe.

THE RAILINGS

Montagu House had had a high impenetrable wall. An attempt to include two 12-foot (93.6 m) high granite sections within Smirke's new 'boundary fence' to screen the officers' residences from the public gaze was favoured by the staff but not carried out following considerable opposition from the public, who complained at the high cost (£24,000) of catering to the whim of the 'parvenu would-be aristocrats'.

Sydney Smirke prepared a number of drawings and, once these had been approved, models for the railings were undertaken by an artist 'of considerable talent' called Lovarti who, inconveniently, died before the work was completed. John Evan Thomas, sculptor, of Brecon but then working in London, and Messrs Collman & Davis took over. John Walker of York won the contract for the ironwork. Metal moulds were largely used, although the frieze was of hammered iron. Each half gate, originally operated by means of a windlass, weighs 5 tons. An underground passage gave access to the works for oiling the machinery and pivots. Walker's last illness delayed the casting of the railings, much to the disquiet of the Trustees. Their concern would have increased considerably if they had known that Walker's son, William, later used the mould made for the main railing pillars to cast two lamp-posts for the entrance to York County Hospital.

The granite for the piers and bases of the railings is said to be from quarries in the Ashburton district of Dartmoor, to the east of Haytor Rocks near Bovey Tracy. The gates were first opened to the public on 31 May 1852. The railings appear first to have been painted a bronze colour.

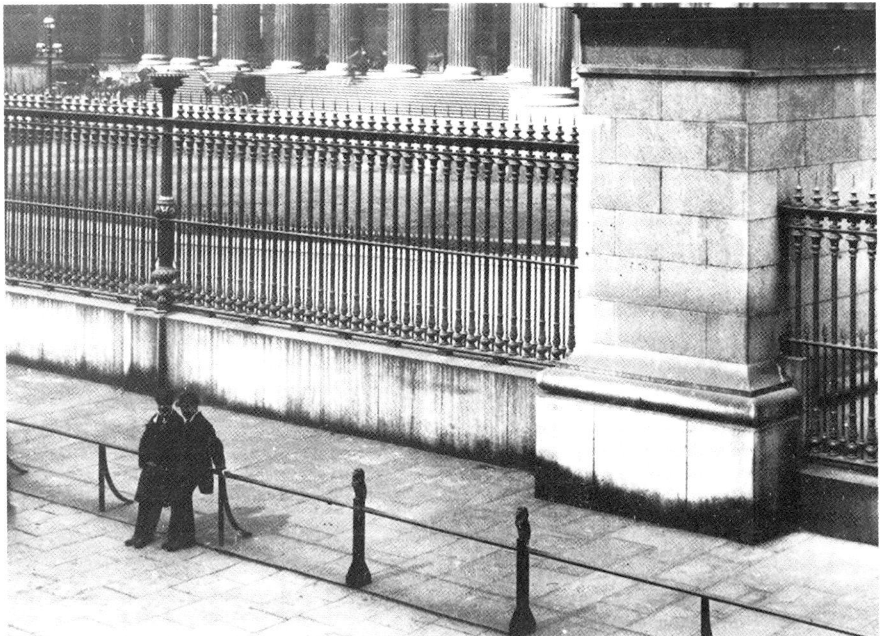

24. *The Museum railings c. 1880. Two contented idlers, only too aware of the photographer, lean against the dwarf railings, providing a suitable scale for Alfred Stevens' cast iron lions (see title page).*

Subsequently they were painted black, then Brunswick green. They are currently 'invisible green'.

The 1675 conveyance of the site to Ralph Montagu had included: 'Alsoe five foote and fower inches of ground in breadth extending the whole front of the said ground abutting upon Great Russell Street . . . to be palleyaded and as a security for the said wall.' In summer 1852 a miniature railing was erected to mark the limits of the Trustees' property . On top of each upright was a miniature lion, the commission for which was given to the sculptor Alfred Stevens. One of Sydney Smirke's pupils recorded later that the architect decided to adopt the sitting lion on the pier at the foot of the great staircase of the Bargello, Florence, producing his own sketch made on the spot many years before as the basis on which the drawing should be made. A clay model was produced by Leonard Collman, and this was altered by Smirke, particularly about the mane and crest.

A total of twenty-five lions sat on the railings until they were dismantled in 1896 to make way for pavement improvements. Messrs Brucciani, a family firm of cast manufacturers in Covent Garden, were given permission to sell copies, which can thus be seen on a number of other London buildings, for example Ely House and the Law Society in Chancery Lane, and there are similar designs on gateposts throughout the country. Twelve of the originals with their connecting lengths of railing were in 1899 transferred to St Paul's Cathedral, where they surround the Wellington Monument which Stevens had designed in 1856; some remain in the Museum.

In 1941 there was a proposal by the Ministry of Supply that the main railings should, as non-essential ironwork, be removed for scrap to help the war effort. Fortunately, common sense prevailed. An automated system for opening the gates was not introduced until the 1970s.

THE RESIDENCES

Since the Museum first moved into Montagu House, senior staff and some servants had been expected to live there, which provided a splendid focus for feuds, petty and otherwise. Smirke designed replacement residences in his two projecting wings: four in the east and three plus apartments in the west, connected to the main building by low corridors. Residence No. 1 – the Principal Librarian's (at the northern end of the East Wing) – is the most elaborate and spacious.

The western residences were constructed first,

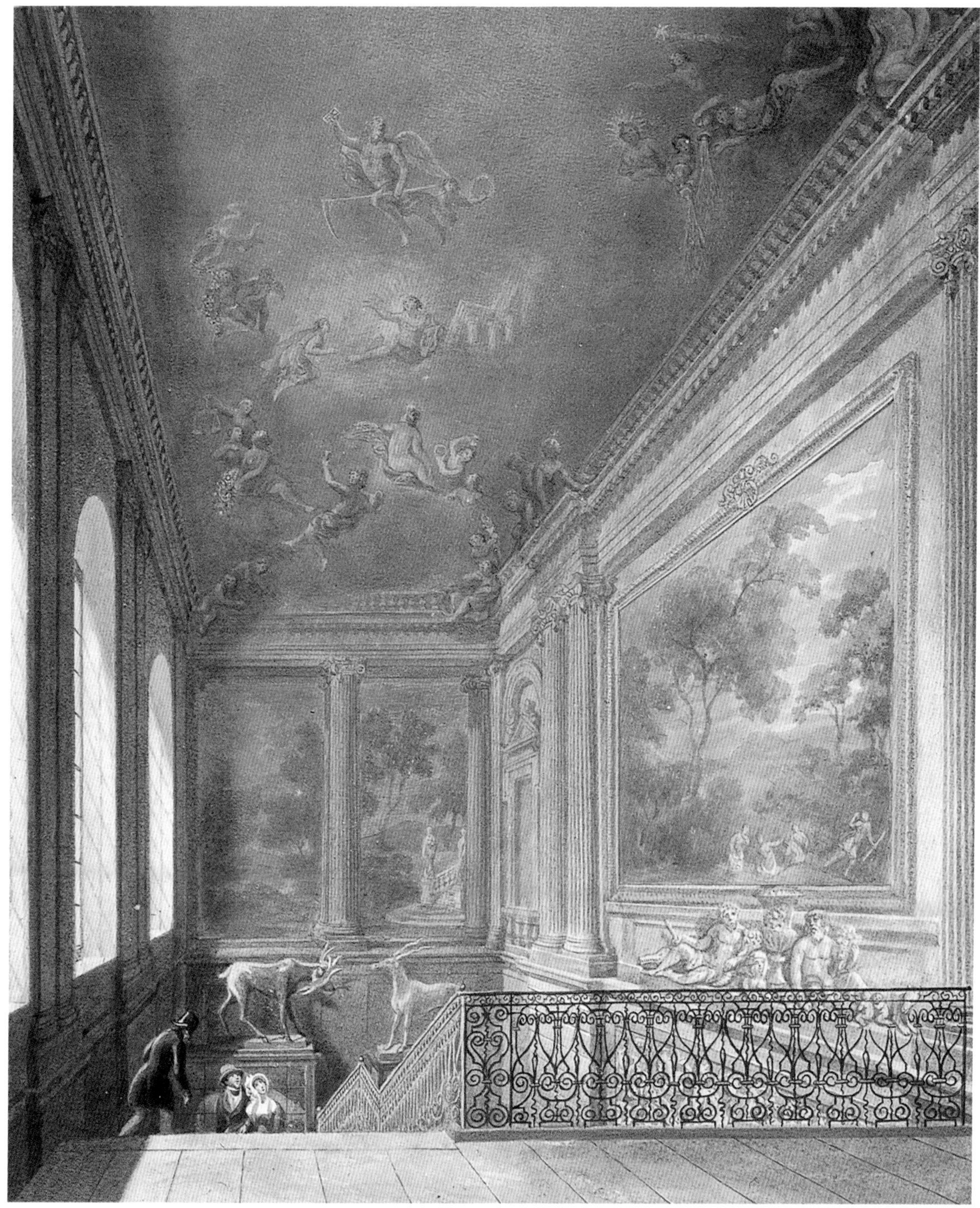

Plate 1 *The Grand Staircase of Montagu House with ceiling frescoes by Charles de la Fosse. 'It is of all the Houses in London, the largest, the completest, and the most magnificent. The stair-case, some of the Apartments and the Ceilings were painted by the celebrated La Fosse, when his genius was in its full vigour; as he was paid with royal munificence, he treated his several subjects with a grandeur worthy of a sovereign's palace. . .' (Pierre Grosley,* Observations on England and its Inhabitants, *1772).*

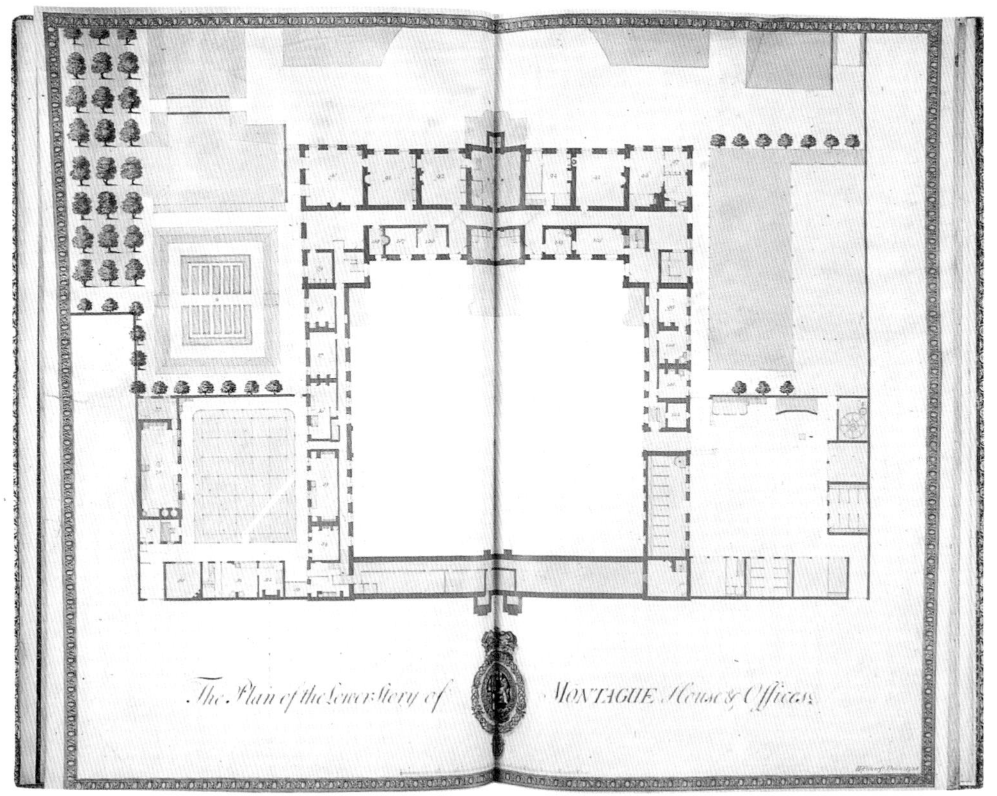

Plate 2 *'The plan of the Lower Story . . .' from a finely bound volume of plans of Montagu House by Henry Flitcroft, 1725. His attention to detail offers a faithful record of the layout of the mansion and its gardens during the time of the 2nd Duke of Montagu. Perhaps it was Flitcroft's time in Bloomsbury that led him, some years later, to name his own house (in Frognal, Hampstead) 'Montagu Grove'.*

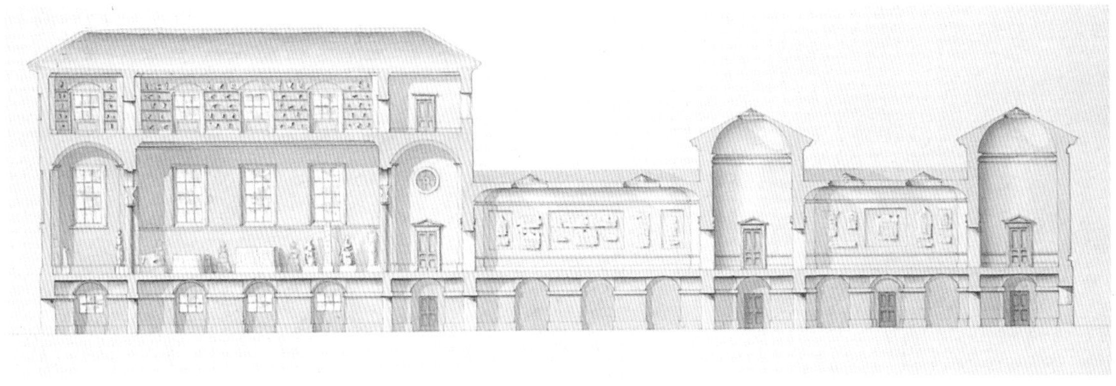

Plate 3 *Elevation of the Townley Gallery by George Saunders, showing the proposed arrangement of 'recent' acquisitions, many clearly identifiable.*

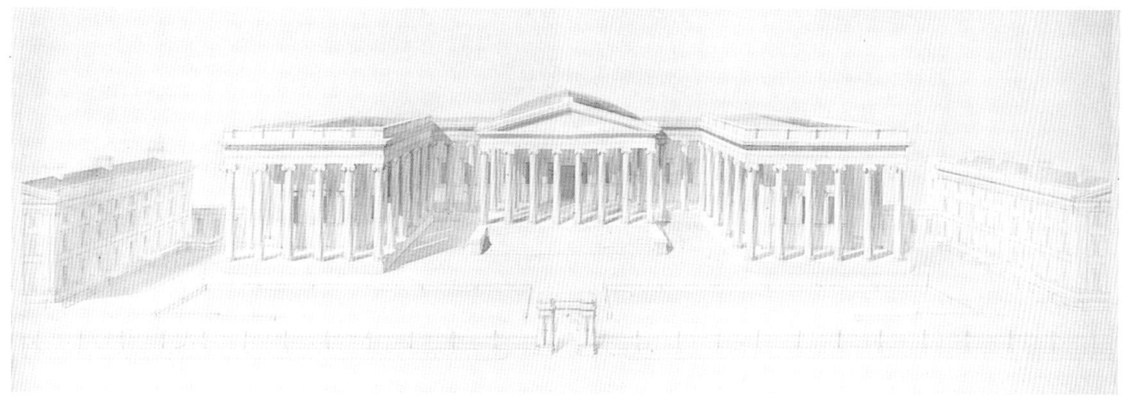

Plate 4 *Panoramic view of the South Front drawn by Sydney Smirke in 1850, showing an early (rejected) design for the forecourt and entrance gates.*

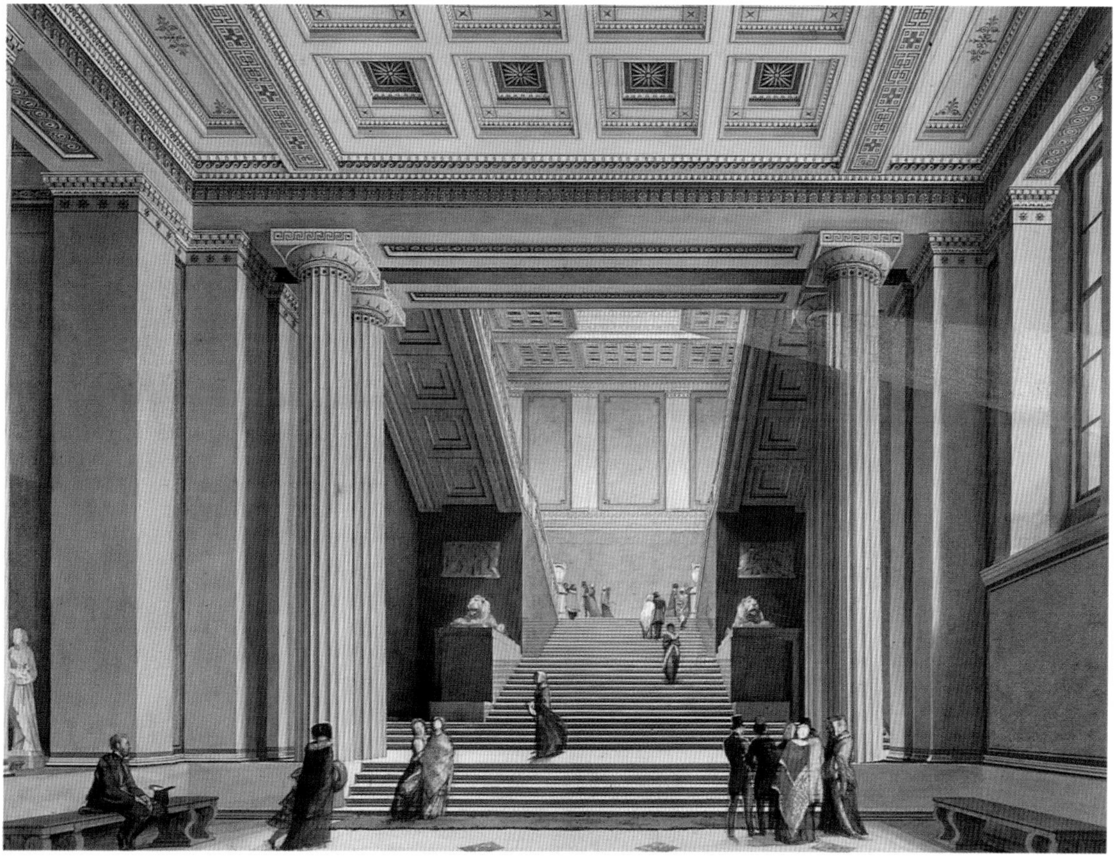

Plate 5 *Watercolour by L. W. Collman showing the polychrome decorative scheme for the Museum's Front Hall and main staircase by Messrs Collman and Davis, 1847.*

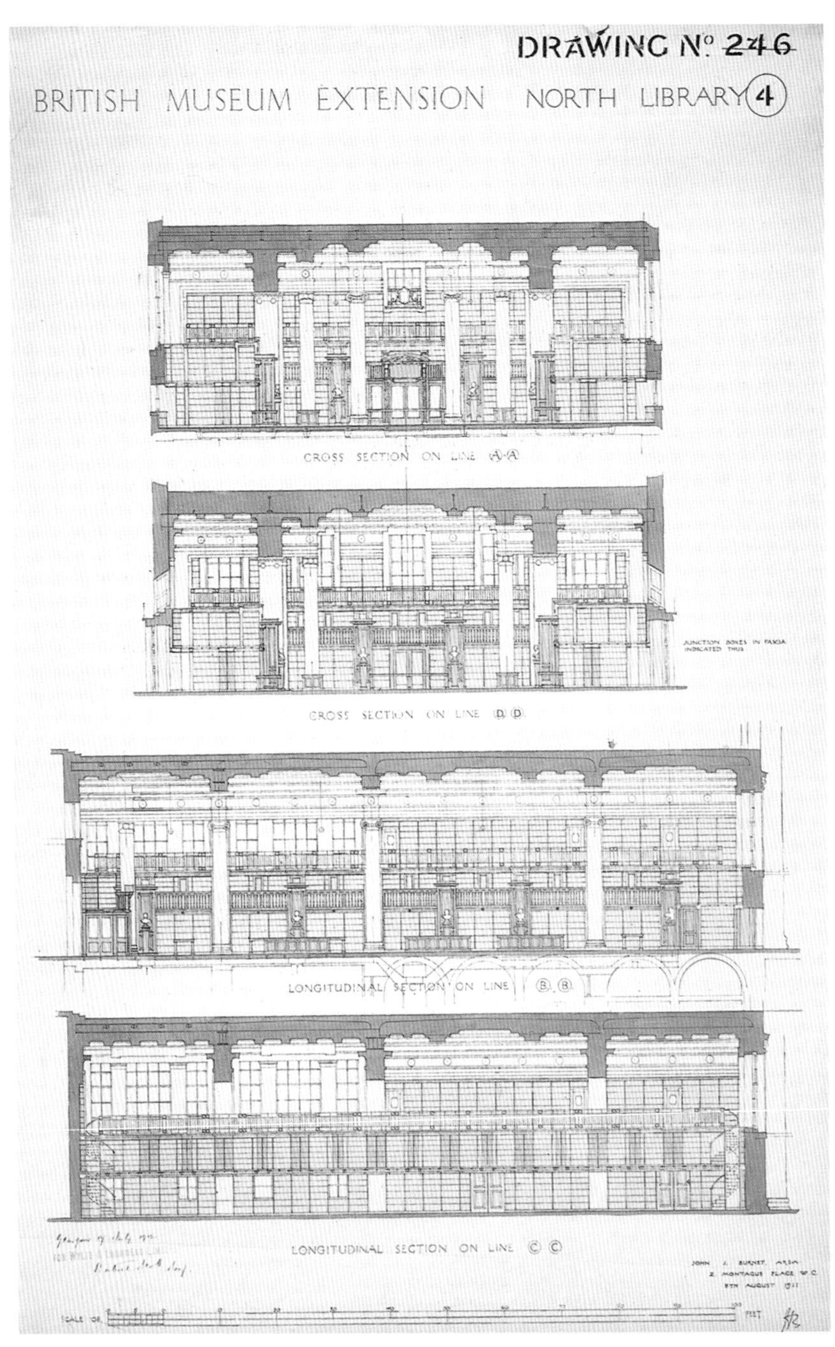

Plate 6 *Detailed elevations of Sir John Burnet's North Library: 'One of the most important rooms in the extension is the North Library, which forms the connecting link between the old and the new buildings on the ground floor. The fittings of this room are of grey-brown oak. The upper balcony of this room, which gives on to the main staircase, has a gilded and enamelled coat of arms flanked by the Royal initials. . . '* (The Times, *11 November 1913).*

being completed in 1846. Smirke made the mistake of making one slightly larger than the others. When designing the eastern block he was obliged 'to enlarge the two central houses in order to remove any cause for the complaint made by Mr Hawkins as to their being inferior to that occupied by Mr Gray, although that inferiority consisted only in the want of a small closet upon each floor.' The eastern range was hastily completed in 1848.

The residences attracted particular criticism from the *Builder* (1843): 'This, to our view, is the besetting defect of Sir Robert Smirke's design. He brings parlours and bedrooms, or apartments of similar inferior purpose and distinction, where they should by no means be made to appear.'

Here until after the Second World War staff and their families were born, lived and died. The residence of the immensely wealthy curator Augustus Wollaston Franks, who established the collections of British and Medieval Antiquities and Ethnography – No. 6 (west) – was 'itself something of a museum, receiving as it did a constant influx of objects bought with his private means; it was also a place frequented by many remarkable men of British and foreign origin who shared his interests and formed the circle of his friends.' Robert Gunther, son of Albert Gunther (1830-1914), Keeper of Zoology, recalled that with his cousin Hermann he would play cricket on the lawns in the forecourt, after the Museum closed at five

25. *Photograph of the drawing room in the Director's Residence (West Residence, No. 6) in 1968, when occupied by Sir Frank Francis, Director 1959-68. Traditionally, the Director's house was Residence No.1. However, Sir George Hill, who had lived in Residence No. 6 since 1912 as Keeper of Coins and Medals, was too attached to his house and remained there on his appointment as Director in 1931. During the summer evenings he could be seen playing bowls on the west lawn.*

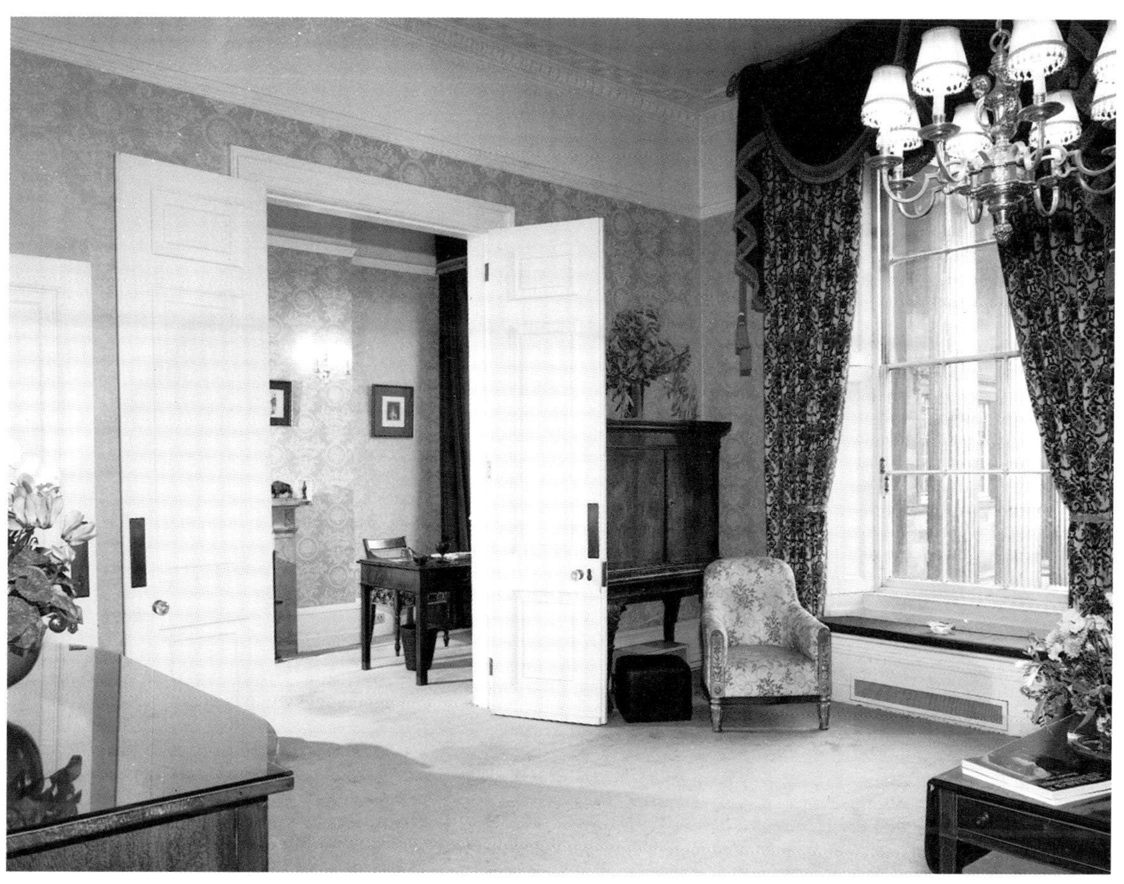

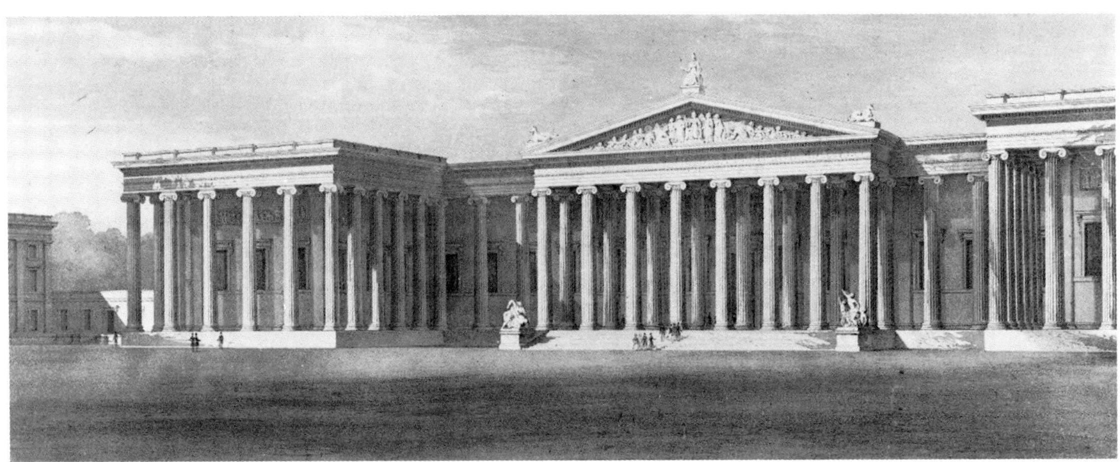

o'clock, 'where Mr Franks, later Sir Wollaston Franks, who lived in the next door house, used to exercise his hobby of keeping the grass free of daisies'. Olive Garnett, daughter of the Keeper of Printed Books, whose residence was traditionally that in the centre of the east side facing Montague Street (No. 2), left an account in her diaries of life in the Museum at the end of the last century. When the public had gone the families had the Museum virtually to themselves. Here were tea parties and *conversazioni*, young ladies exercising in the 'rangle' and preparing for balls, conversations on the 'grass plot' with anarchists, and not a little scandal.

Staff began to move out of the residences between the wars, finding it difficult to obtain servants and preferring smaller houses. The Director's Residence, now in the West Wing, is still occupied, but the others are now largely used as offices.

SCULPTURE

A correspondent in the *Builder* wrote in 1858, 'We seem to have a strange propensity in London for putting up pedestals and leaving them unoccupied.' The British Museum has demonstrated this well. A close inspection reveals thirty or more plinths still awaiting occupants.

In May 1847 Sydney Smirke suggested to the Trustees that statues might be considered for the tympanum and acroteria of the pediment, the pedestals at the base of the portico and at the foot of the great staircase, plus bas-reliefs near the same

26. *Sydney Smirke's impression of the completed south front of the Museum, 1851: ' . . . the frieze will bear an inscription; the tympanum of the pediment will be filled with appropriate sculpture; upon its apex will be seated our tutelar national representative [i.e. Britannia]; and at the two other extremities will be equine figures. The steps to the portico will also be flanked with noble groups of sculpture' (Madden scrapbooks, British Library). Funds were available for the tympanum sculptures only.*

place, over the great door and under the colonnade. Artists' impressions of the south front at this time show what might be Britannia on the central acroterion with something reminiscent of Laocoon struggling at either side of the front steps. In the event, given that all these sculptures would have cost £6,000 and the Trustees had a mere £3,000 available, only the tympanum received its decoration. There are only partial records of what was proposed elsewhere. In September 1846 Sydney Smirke suggested for the granite pedestals at the foot of the stairs two colossal lions, possibly the 'Prudhoe' lions or restored copies. In March 1848 there is a suggestion of 'allegorical figures representing commerce and agriculture . . . or Art and Science' on the pedestals. Shakespeare, Bacon, Milton and Newton were specifically proposed for the plinths between the railings, and models for two of these were submitted to the Trustees in July 1850 by Richard Westmacott.

A frieze of undressed blocks of stone can be seen running along the front behind the colonnade. In 1846 a correspondent of the *Builder* suggested that 'a sculptured frieze, expressive of the uses and objects of the building' be introduced in this space.

Two white marble fountains with lions' heads, designed by Sydney Smirke junior, were erected to either side of the Front Door or, as Sir Frederic Madden, the irascible Keeper of Manuscripts, put it: '22 September 1859 Workmen defaced the entrance of the BM by erecting two drinking fountains. Let the public drink, but surely not at the immediate entrance to a large public building, where a dirty mess is sure to be made!'

Sir Richard Westmacott (1775-1856) had long been involved with the Museum, having advised on the arrangement of sculptures in the Townley Gallery as early as 1805 and on subsequent displays, irritating keepers and the architect. He was now commissioned to produce the sculpture for the tympanum, and in June 1848 put forward proposals. Sydney Smirke, a practical architect, advised the Trustees to obtain a written contract, with a penalty for delay. Westmacott, the artist, apprised of this, took considerable umbrage and wrote: '. . . the draft you have sent me would form an admirable Railway contract but your solicitors do not understand Art or they would not have proposed the penalty of weeks. If however the Trustees should insist on that change pray instruct them to insert 1852 for 1851. I object also to be placed under the architect he might annoy me very much . . . .'

Westmacott provided, reluctantly, a brief note of his scheme (fifteen statues and fourteen accessories) which represented the 'Progress of Civilisation', beginning at the western end with

27. *A photograph by Roger Fenton of the south front of the British Museum in 1857, showing the pedimental sculpture by Richard Westmacott, installed during 1851. This photograph was a gift of the British Museum Society.*

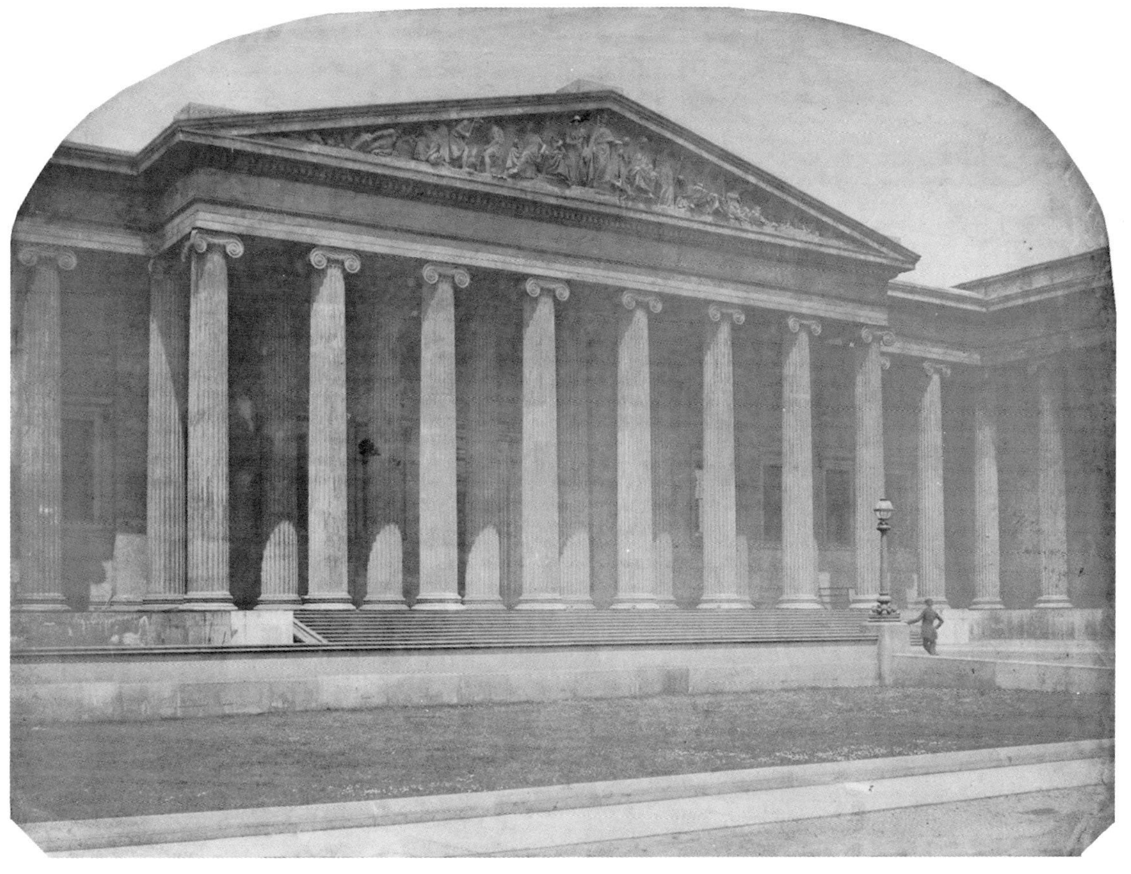

man 'emerging from a rude savage state through the influence of Religion' to become 'a Hunter and a Tiller of the Earth, and labouring for his subsistence'. For some time paganism prevails. The keystone of the composition is Astronomy 'as studied by the Egyptians, Chaldaeans and other nations'. Civilization has made considerable progress and so as the composition descends towards the east, Mathematics appears 'in allusion to Science being now pursued on known sound principles' and Drama, Poetry, and Music balance the group of the Fine Arts on the western side. At the far eastern end is Natural History.

Westmacott appears to have achieved the 1851 deadline, for on 19 April 1851 a correspondent to the *Builder* reported: 'They were hoisting 'Mathematics' when we were there – a sitting figure of 7 or 8 tons weight. The central statue, standing, is "Astronomy" and is around 12 feet [3.6 m] high.'

At one time there was some uncertainty as to whether the blue background shown in a drawing of the sculptures (now in the Museum) had or had not been executed, particularly since this was not apparent during stone cleaning in 1978. There were, however, a number of contemporary references, such as that in the *Art Journal* which stated: 'There is a peculiarity in the frieze which at once strikes the observer, that is, the composition being relieved by colour – blue; this is an imitation of the Parthenon.' The puzzle was solved when the pedimental sculptures were cleaned and repaired in 1992 and traces of blue paint, no doubt rapidly obscured by Victorian pollution and forgotten, were discovered.

THE ASSYRIAN GALLERIES

The sculptures discovered in the Museum's excavations at the Assyrian cities of Nimrud and Nineveh between 1845 and 1854 were a tremendous revelation to the Victorians, particularly those who saw in them the prospect of the Bible vindicated. To the Trustees, however, they were something of an embarrassment. The building of the Museum, according to Smirke's plans, had just been more or less finished. Yet some 300 slabs, some weighing several tons, were on their way and had to be accommodated in a hurry. The first pieces arrived in June 1847.

In 1850 Smirke produced a sketch of the western area showing where additional galleries to receive the Assyrian sculptures might be placed. This would upset the chronological arrangement of the classical sculptures, but the public were anxious to see these wonders. Although part of the space had been intended for a Prints and Drawings gallery, the sculptures were installed in the southern side gallery in 1852 and in 1854 in the northern side gallery, both parallel to the West Wing, and also in the 'Assyrian transept' at the end of the Egyptian Sculpture Gallery.

In 1857-8 the 'Assyrian Basement Room' was constructed to the west of the Nimrud Gallery. The Assyrian Basements were remodelled between 1893 and 1894: the sculptures were raised to ground-floor level and a light gallery carried round the room, described as being 'like a swimming bath'. The Lion Hunt of Ashurbanipal was viewed by visitors walking round it supported on an iron cat-walk (see fig. 38). A lecture theatre was part of the 1890s reconstruction.

In spite of the Keeper of Antiquities describing these galleries in 1853 as 'only an expedient and not a very good one', the narrow rooms on the ground floor remain today. The appearance of other ground-floor Assyrian galleries was altered in the 1960s and major alterations took place in the basement.

THE SMIRKE COURTYARD

Robert Smirke had high hopes for the courtyard at the centre of the Museum. There would be elaborate porticos on all four sides and a linking route along the North Wing, bypassing the closed library areas. Here visitors could promenade, and it would be possible, as in Montagu House, to grow botanical plants. However, in 1833 Smirke was obliged to cut back on his plans due to shortage of funds. The porticos were reduced in size and made ornamental rather than functional. When the Front Hall was opened in 1847 there was for the public no access to the courtyard, which was visible only through a single glazed panel in a massive oak door. One complaining journalist wrote in the *Builder* of 1853 of '. . . its grass plots being now only frequented by the cats of the neighbourhood, and the silence of its solitude only broken by their cries'.

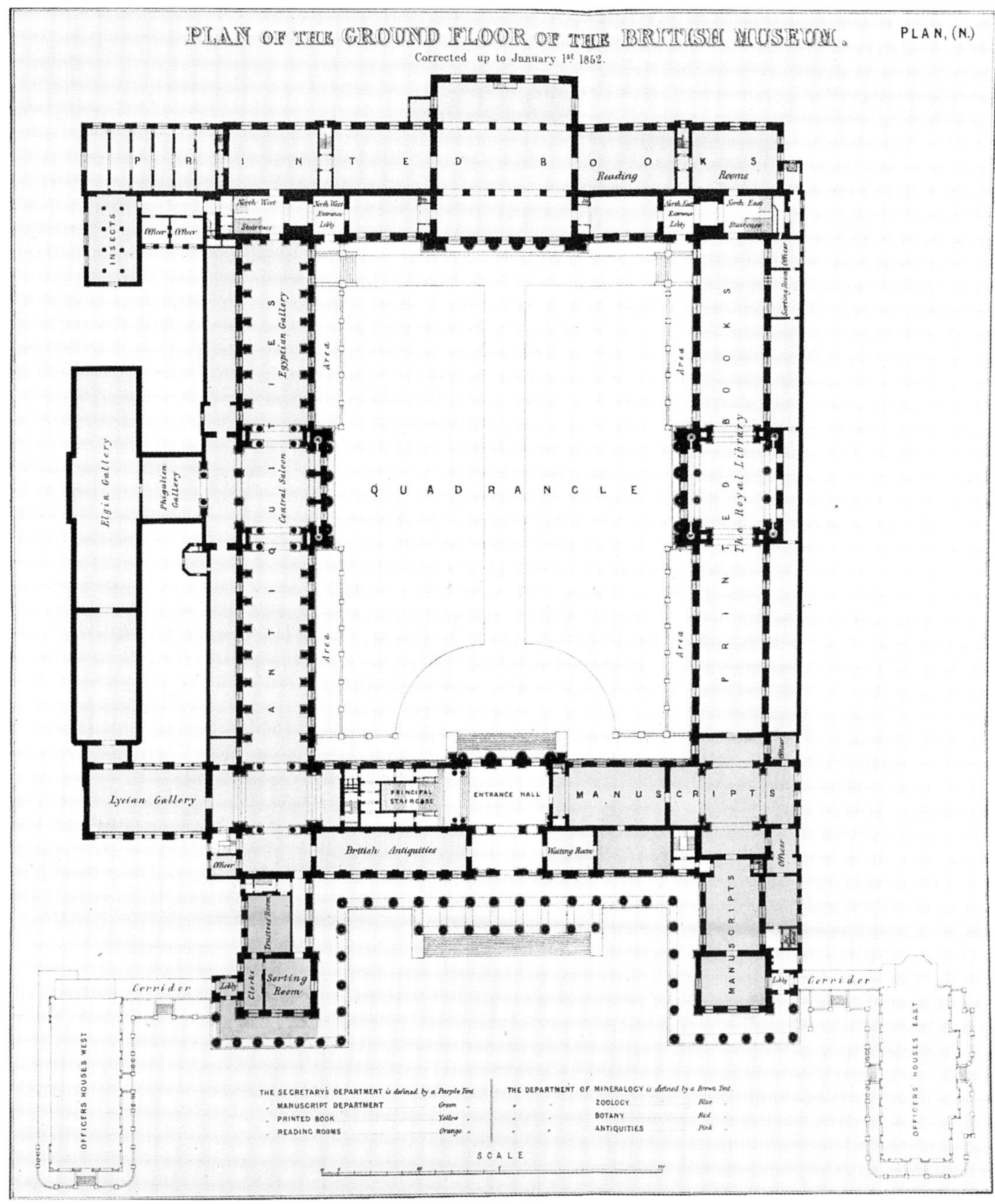

28. *Lithograph plan of the Ground Floor of the Museum published in June 1852 and 'corrected up to January 1852'. This was used within a Trustees' publication on the need for additional accommodation in the Museum. The quadrangle appears ripe for development.*

But perhaps this disdain for the centre of Smirke's plan was not entirely removed from the fact that eyes had already been cast on this tempting area. Suggestions had first appeared in a series of papers in the *Mechanics' Magazine* for 1836 and 1837, written, anonymously, by Thomas Watts (then Assistant in the Department of Printed

Books). William Hosking, Professor of Architecture in the University of London, also published a pamphlet on the subject in 1850, proposing that the northern half of the King's Library be turned into a reading room, with a domed rotunda in the courtyard for the display of sculpture and other antiquities.

It is not improbable that the Museum authorities' failure to provide public access to the courtyard was linked to the realisation that the space would have to be used for Museum purposes. As the Smirke building went up, the collections increased beyond all expectations. For example, the library under the leadership of Antonio Panizzi grew from 150,000 volumes in 1827 to 520,000 in 1856 and was to exceed a million in fifteen years; natural history had expanded ten-fold since the beginning of the century; Layard was busily excavating in Assyria; the classical archaeologists had much more to discover; and prehistory, ethnography and the British collections were about to expand beyond all recognition.

Panizzi (1797-1879) was a dominating figure in the Museum during the mid-nineteenth century. Condemned to death for revolutionary activity in his native Italy, he arrived in England in 1823 with little command of the English language, but his abilities and particularly his talent for enlisting powerful patronage led to his appointment to the Museum in 1831, promotion to Keeper of Printed Books in 1837 and to Principal Librarian in 1856. Some of the Museum's space problems were exacerbated by his ruthless enforcement of the Copyright Acts and his determination to establish the finest library in the world.

Panizzi's first rough sketch for a new reading room was drawn on 18 April 1852 and a more finished version was produced by an assistant, Charles Cannon. This was laid before the Trustees on 5 May and approved in principle. Panizzi's proposal incorporated several concentric galleries, supported on cast iron columns, covered with coved glazing and surrounded by a rectangular bookstack. Sydney Smirke refined this and suggested a dome and glazed vaulting with a more architectural treatment to the interior. The Treasury was initially reluctant but, Panizzi having obtained the support of the Prime Minister (Lord Aberdeen), £61,000, a first instalment for the work, was voted by Parliament on 3 July 1854.

The Great Court project will include major developments below the courtyard; on the north side will be the Sainsbury African Galleries and on the south the extensive Clore Centre for Education with the Hugh and Catherine Stevenson Theatre.

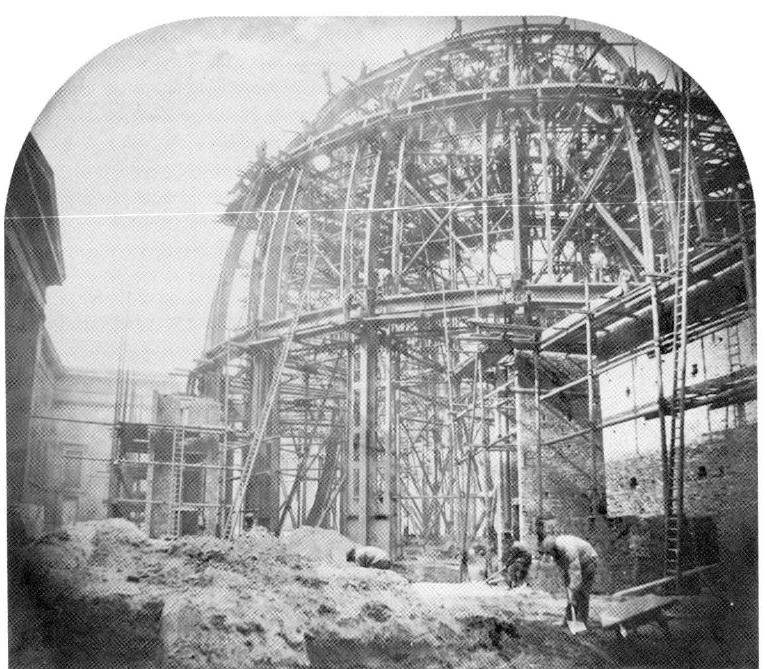

29. *'The intricate and complex scaffolding, and the works in progress in the Quadrangle now present an appearance so picturesque and, I think, so remarkable, that I am induced to suggest whether the Photographer to the Museum might not be employed to obtain a record...' Sydney Smirke, no doubt proud of his work, convinced the Trustees of the worth of such a record for posterity. The Museum's first official photographer, Roger Fenton, was away in the Crimea (his first contract at the Museum being at an end), so William Lake Price was asked to take photographs during the spring and summer of 1855.*

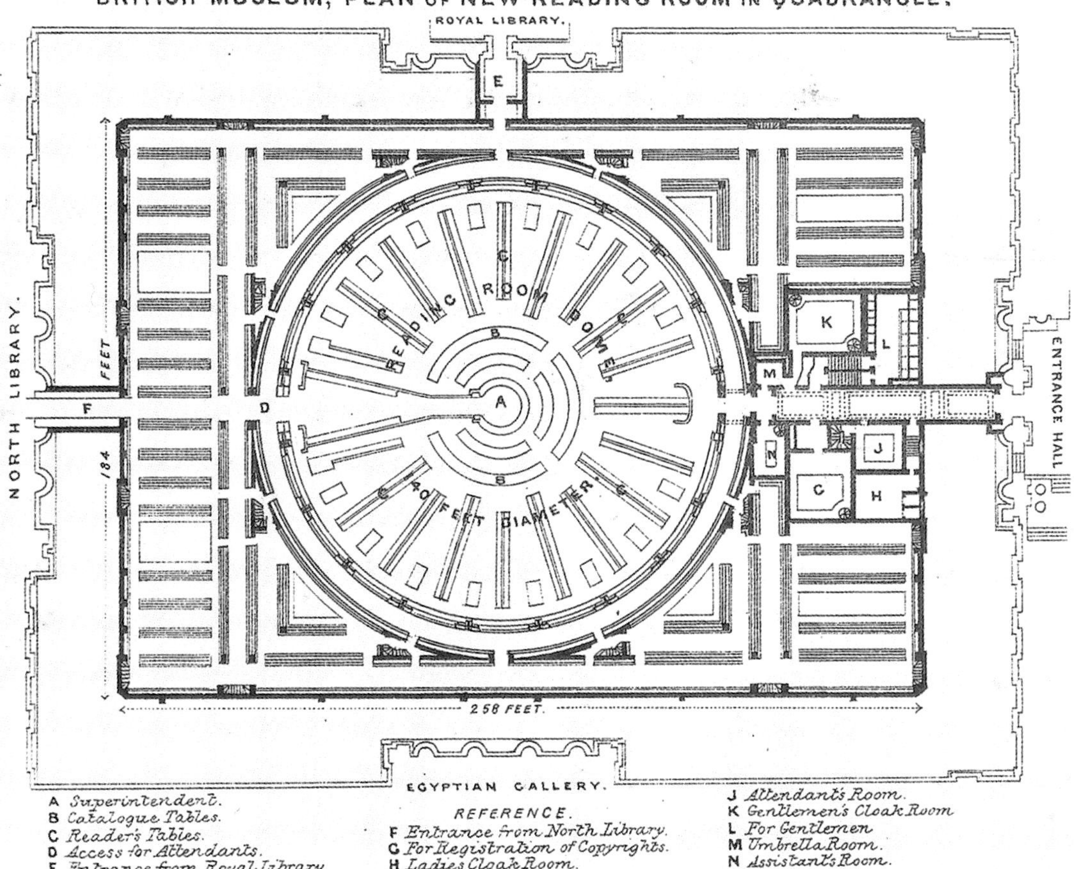

30. *Plan of the Round Reading Room and adjacent bookstacks. This plan was printed on the reverse of an invitation card for a private view of the Reading Room on 5 May 1857.*

THE CONSTRUCTION OF THE ROUND READING ROOM

The speed with which the project was completed is astounding. Work started in May 1854; in September the first brick was laid; in January 1855 the first iron standard erected. On 2 June 1855 the scaffolding was removed, and in September the dome was covered with copper. Readers were admitted in May 1857.

The Round Reading Room – the seventh in the Museum's history – is immense, its sheer scale only now revealed by the demolition of its surrounding bookstacks. The dome is 140 feet (42.6 m) in diameter, only 2 feet (60 cm) less than the dome of the Pantheon in Rome. It is a further example of the pioneering use of cast iron. There are twenty iron piers each in three sections. These were not fitted together; instead gaps were left between the castings and filled with 'rust cement', a paste invented by William Murdoch (1754-1839) which swelled as it set. The inner lining of the dome is papier mâché, ⅝ inch (15 mm) thick.

The original arrangement accommodated 302 readers at thirty-five tables radiating out from the key-hole shaped catalogue desk like a spider's web – indeed, the space below the Reading Room with its heating ducts was known as 'The Spider'. The tables were originally padded and covered with black leather and Panizzi had recommended for each reader 'as comfortable a chair as could be wished'. The floor was covered with 'kamptulicon' (a mixture of rubber, gutta percha and cork on a canvas backing) to reduce noise. The room was decorated in azure blue and cream with elegant gilding.

In 1880 the small tables between the main reading desks were lengthened to provide an extra 62 seats, and free-standing bookcases were added. The original black leather was replaced by blue in the 1960s. In the 1950s the table (opposite the southern entrance) was removed, as were later two others. The Reading Room was redecorated in 1907, 1951-2 and 1963-4. The subsequent schemes were not unlike the first, although the 1907 scheme by John James Burnet, in gold and white, incorporated nineteen great names in English literature (all male and now deleted) in the breastwork of the windows. In August 1937 the Daily Telegraph *described an unofficial scheme devised by a regular reader, Dr Clement (and developed by architect Frederick Etchells). Mottled green walls and bright green varnish with a floodlit dome, they believed, would prove psychologically beneficial. The scheme was not taken up.*

Statues and paintings

In a report to the Trustees on 10 August 1854 Panizzi proposed that:

> ... proper steps be taken to induce the government to approve of the interior part of the cupola over the new Reading Room being painted in a high art style suited to such a place . . . whether the painting should be in oil or tempera, would be a matter for future consideration . . . This seems to Mr Panizzi a rare or rather unique opportunity, which ought to be eagerly seized, for encouraging that taste for the arts which is now so popular.

The Trustees declined 'under existing circumstances' to recommend the scheme to the Treasury. Panizzi, in a further report dated 12 October 1854, pointed out that use could be made of scaffolding already in place but if the work were delayed it could never be accomplished because of disruption to readers. He also expressed the hope that the architect would be directed to make preparations for the placing of marble statues between the windows in the cupola. Smirke incorporated the necessary plinths but does not seem to have had a particular enthusiasm for the project.

Alfred Stevens, a friend of Panizzi, constructed a model (now in the Victoria and Albert Museum) showing the distribution across each of the twenty bays of the dome of decorative paintings featuring 'branches of man's creative achievement'. An engineer (Volprignano) is said to have produced a system of scaffolding in 1864 designed to allow the work to be completed without disturbing the readers, but the Trustees, certainly on financial grounds and possibly from inclination, ignored the proposals and only a bust of Panizzi by Carlo Marochetti, subscribed by staff, was erected at the entrance in 1857. In 1925 Sigismund Goetze revived the idea of elaborate paintings, producing a scheme to be executed at his own expense. The Royal Fine Art Commission vetoed the 13-foot-high (4 m) figures and the 'bright and vivacious colours', although Goetze was only told politely by the Trustees that 'that they are not in favour of adopting any but the simplest form of Decoration for the dome of the Reading Room'.

The Reading Room was and is breathtaking and must have been particularly so when first seen. The *Publishers' Circular* later described it as '. . . a circular temple of marvellous dimensions, rich in blue, and white, and gold'. However, Frederic Madden, who detested Panizzi, noted in his diary (Friday 17 April 1857) that the 'gilded dome' was 'utterly unfitted for the real purposes of study . . . a monstrous example of the abuse of influence'.

The Reading Room, having been vacated by the British Library (p. 73), will revert as nearly as possible to its original appearance with the removal of the twentieth-century accretions and the restoration of the original colour scheme. It will house the Walter and Leonore Annenberg Centre and the Paul Hamlyn Library.

The bookstacks

At the time of the construction of the Reading Room the use of electricity for lighting had not been developed and gas lighting was strictly prohibited in the Museum because of the danger of fire. An ingenious solution to maximize book storage was devised, namely bookstacks of perforated iron supplied by Pontifex. These were built in the rectangular area around the dome. The stacks, known as the 'Iron Library', contained three linear miles (4.8 km) of bookcases, eight feet (2.4 m) high, in which were set an estimated twenty-five miles (40 km) of shelves, adjustable by means of brass pins for which 2,750,000 holes were provided. An innovative measure, in 1889, to increase

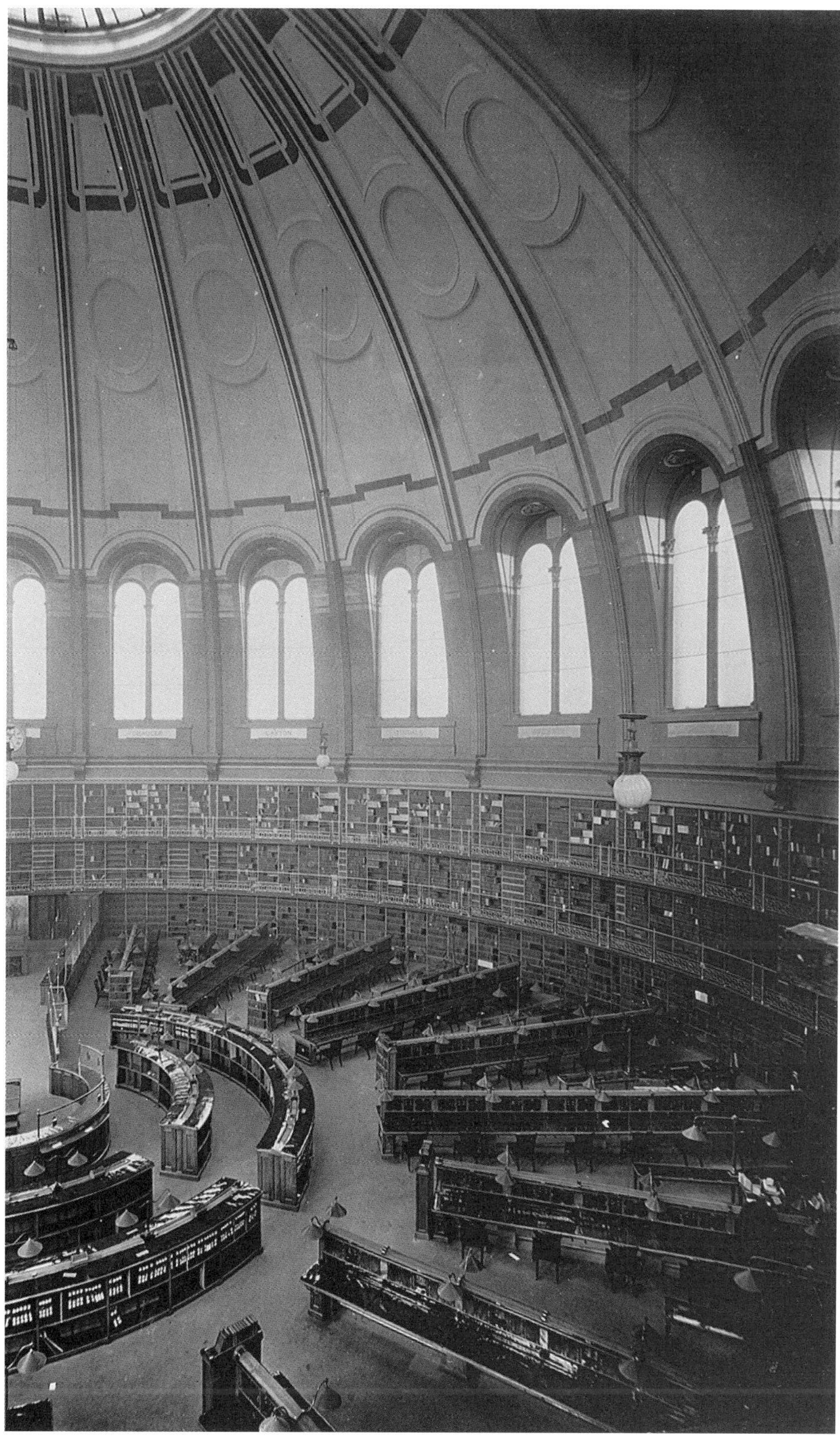

31. *The Round Reading Room from the south gallery, soon after Sir John Burnet's 1907 redecoration. Burnet's 'very simple scheme' was introduced to 'increase the apparent height and lightness of the dome' by 'treating it as one mass'. It was painted white and relieved by lines of bright gold to the ribs, around the heads of the windows and skylight. By the 1930s it was reduced to 'elephant grey and sooty gold . . . a depressing effect'.*

shelf space (the construction of sliding presses in front of the original presses) was initially successful. However, the huge increase in weight proved too much and they were later removed.

Major changes occurred during the twentieth century (p. 63). All the bookstacks have now been demolished for the construction of the Great Court; the iron framework of the south-east (the only original one remaining, although much altered) has been preserved.

REFRESHMENT ROOMS

In 1866 the Trustees opened a Public Refreshment Room in the basement at the bottom of the stairs from the the Third Graeco-Roman Saloon. The *Civil Service Gazette* gave it a rapturous reception:

> The princes of Thebes, lying in their perfumed coffins, are forgotten in the glories of roast beef; Isis and Sesostris vanish to oblivion before the more potent attraction of college-pudding; the kings of Nineveh, engaged with frantic enthusiasm for the chase, fade from the memory in the vapoury presence of boiled cabbage! . . . The educational tendency of the Museum will lose none of its force by giving the minds unaccustomed to much exertion an opportunity for rest and refreshment.

The Refreshment Room was ill-managed, and after complaints from readers and staff it closed in 1870. There were subsequent attempts to provide refreshments. At one point these were supplied on the upper floor at the north-east corner of the building, but in 1887 a larger room was opened off the centre of the Egyptian Sculpture Gallery. The restaurant then returned to the basement below the old Third Graeco-Roman Room, and it was here that in 1965 the problem of boiled cabbage smells returned to the galleries (perhaps it never went away). The Ministry of Works, convinced that 'no equipment existed which could eliminate these smells', installed an industrial 'Airwick' at the foot of the restaurant stairs.

A greatly improved purpose-built restaurant was located in the New Wing development (pp. 68-9). Restaurant facilities will move to the Great Court.

COLOUR SCHEMES

One matter that exercised the nineteenth-century Trustees was the question of colour on the walls of the Museum. There are indications that Montagu House was painted in light colours. Certainly the great hall was in 1807 painted plain stone, and Richard Westmacott junior in 1858 recalled that, 'The Old Townley Galleries, as I remember them many years ago, were painted a light grey, granite colour.' Sir Robert Smirke stated in 1833 of the new Egyptian Sculpture Gallery: 'What I should much prefer myself would be no other color than that of *Stone* – for we have no other superfluous quantity of light in the Centre Gallery and any other color like that given to the Greek Rooms would be ruinously dark.' In 1832 he had written, 'I am *innocent* of the selection of colors that have been laid on the walls of the Greek Rooms . . . There will be no small trouble and difficulty in cleaning the walls of the heavy staining matter that has been laid upon them.' He was, however, not entirely opposed to ornament, for an 1832 drawing of a ceiling in the West Wing shows a simple design of a star within each coffered section.

In 1840 it was noted that, 'The saloons containing the Elgin and Phigalian marbles have lately, after a variety of trials, been coloured in imitation of rose-coloured Egyptian porphyry, and the roof of grayish granite.'

The Front Hall (opened 1847) was decorated in an elaborate polychrome scheme, although Sydney Smirke hesitated to insist that this should also be applied to the galleries. When Robert Smirke's Egyptian Sculpture Gallery was completed by Sydney Smirke in 1850, the original light stone was superseded by dark colours. The scheme was described by the *Builder* in 1851:

> The ceiling of the new galleries, is formed, like those of the other galleries, into a series of small deeply-sunk panels; the ground of these is coloured blue, and upon this, in the centre of each, is a gilt star, or a composition of four honeysuckles, placed alternately. The plaster bed-moulds around each panel have red in them, and on the soffit of the main beams, forming the larger divisions of the ceiling, panels are formed by green lines. The frieze on the walls has a white honeysuckle pattern on a quiet green ground; but

> where it runs out over the projecting piers, frets are substituted for the honeysuckle. The upper part of the walls is coloured sage green, with panels formed by red lines, and the lower part (the podium) is to be coloured dark red, as a background for the sculptures.

Apart from questions of taste, the nineteenth-century arguments, particularly in the absence of electricity, revolved round the best method of showing off the sculptures, and in 1859 the request to the Trustees from the Keeper of Antiquities, Edward Hawkins, to paint the small Graeco-Roman Saloon raised the question of colour for all the Museum's sculpture galleries. The subject was discussed at some length. Hawkins, who preferred the dark scheme, recalled that when the Elgin Room was first opened the walls were painted in a very delicate colour and that this had led to complaints from the public, since the sculptures appeared dirty by contrast. The Trustees' current artistic adviser, Richard Westmacott junior (1799-1872), who had succeeded his father, continued instead to advocate light colours which would counteract the darkness of the London atmosphere and which had been successful in 'certain Drawing Rooms in private houses'. The darker scheme more suited the taste of the times, and Trustees decided in 1859 that 'the general colour of the walls of the sculpture galleries should be red'.

There was occasional repainting and cleaning, but this basically dark colour scheme with decorative mouldings, in some instances becoming decidedly dingy with age, lasted until the 1930s. Perhaps a hint of change came in 1902 when the Egyptian Sculpture Gallery was repainted – as before, but with white introduced into wall spaces flanking the windows to provide better lighting for the exhibits.

In the 1930s came a change of style when pastel shades were introduced. As the *Evening News* put it:

> Gradually the dull red with which generations of Londoners have been familiar is to give way to delicate blends of greys, blues, mauves and greens. For it has been found that the art works often centuries or so BC are best shown in an ultra-modern colour setting such as might be found in a fashionable West End drawing-room.

THE FRONT HALL EXTENSION

In 1875 a correspondent to the *Builder* exclaimed with horror, 'Is it really true that the Trustees are about to pull down the present magnificent staircase, perhaps the grandest staircase to any public building in England?' It was. To solve the Museum's perennial space problems the Trustees, unprepared to let sentiment stand in the way of more space, had come to an agreement with the Treasury to demolish the great staircase. The suggestion had first emerged in 1862 and had been put to the Treasury in 1868. There was a delay, but on 4 November 1874 the plan was put forward to provide ground and upper floor galleries for classical antiquities by removing the principal staircase and erecting two staircases on unoccupied space to the north of the entrance hall.

Funds were authorized by the Treasury in February 1875. However, at the last minute, in July 1875, further schemes were proposed, including one which would save the staircase. This was accepted and a new two-level extension, in style and decoration matching the rest of the Front Hall, designed by Sir John Taylor, was completed in summer 1877, but at the expense of Smirke's fine inner southern portico. The floor above – the Prehistoric Saloon – was allocated to British and Medieval Antiquities.

The upper floor was very badly damaged in 1941 but rebuilt in 1964-5. This extension has now been demolished to make way for the Great Court and the restoration of Smirke's southern portico.

THE PRESSURE FOR SPACE

There is a pre-metric proverb that 'you cannot fit a quart into a pint pot'. This sums up much of the Museum's architectural history. As early as 1850 'Zeta' was writing in the *Builder*, 'It is somewhat strange that the architect of the Museum did not so plan the buildings originally as to provide for the contingency – not an improbable one even at that time – of later additions being required.' A Royal Commission on the Museum reported in 1850 that the building was 'a warning rather than a model to the architect of any additional structure'.

Smirke's building was indeed wholly inadequate for the growing collections. Over the years various options were considered. The Trustees could try to cram more on to the Bloomsbury site (an extra storey on the Smirke building was considered in 1858, as was converting the staff residences); they could buy land in the vicinity for expansion (but this was built over and thus expensive); they could move some of their collections elsewhere; or (an option rather favoured by the Treasury) they could collect less. The Trustees have, however, always adhered to the adage 'a museum which does not collect is a dead museum'.

As early as 1846 the advantages of separating natural history from antiquities and the library were being suggested. In 1856, Professor Richard Owen, Superintendent of the natural history departments, submitted proposals for a move, but the increasingly powerful scientific lobby urged that these collections should remain near the national library. On 21 January 1860, at a Special General Meeting, the Trustees having digested the fact that it had been estimated that the eight acres south of the Museum would cost £455,000 compared with £40,000 in South Kensington, resolved by nine votes to eight to take the cheapest option. Natural history would have to go.

32. *The Mammalian Room in 1875, at the southern end of the East Wing of 1823-8. The circular window originally overlooked the Principal Librarian's garden. It disappeared with the construction of the White Wing around 1883.*

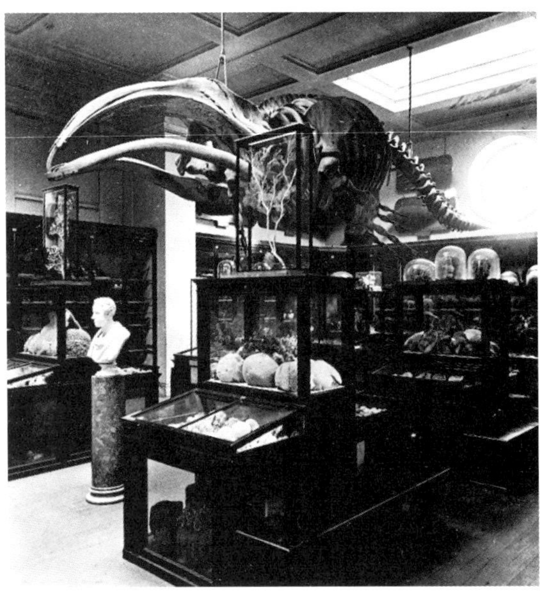

A Select Committee of the House of Commons appointed in May 1860 took a different view and recommended the purchase of the ground immediately surrounding the Museum. This recommendation was, however, without effect; and after some further correspondence the Treasury issued a Minute on 13 November 1861 in which they expressed their opinion that Government alone ought to bear the responsibility of whatever proposals might be made to Parliament and announced their conclusion that some of the collections ought to be removed, and that the Government would be prepared to make proposals to the Commissioners of the Exhibition of 1851 for the provision of adequate space at South Kensington.

These proposals were considered by the Trustees, who finally on 10 February 1862 decided on the removal of the whole of natural history and also ethnography. Further negotiations with the Treasury followed and a Bill was introduced into Parliament to permit the Trustees to transfer the collections out of the building. In 1865 the Trustees accepted a design by Captain Francis Fowke, RE. On Fowke's death the following year the Government's choice fell on Alfred Waterhouse. Various sites were still being considered, but the favourite on grounds of cost remained South Kensington. Plans for a Museum of Natural History were approved in February 1871 and in December 1872 the Treasury accepted Messrs Baker's tender for the construction, within three years and for £35,000, of the building in Cromwell Road. Work started in 1873. The mineralogical, geological and botanical collections had moved by the autumn of 1880. Zoology did not leave until 1883, but the formal opening took place in 1881. As *Punch* had written in 1861 when the move was being discussed:

> Mother Nature, beat retreat,
> Out, M'm, from Great Russell Street!
> Here, in future, folks shall scan
> Nothing but the works of Man.

This was the first departure from the universal ideals of the Museum's founders, although the Trustees retained responsibility for the new museum until 1963.

In addition to the 92,600 square feet (8,547 sq. m) of space already taken up by antiquities in 1868, around 61,500 square feet (5,713 sq. m) now became available at Bloomsbury, although as it was largely on the upper floor it could do little to solve the problem of housing heavy sculptures. Egyptian and Assyrian antiquities took over the upper northern wing, with Greek and Roman extending through the upper western. Ethnography could at last spread itself in the upper eastern gallery, while British and Medieval antiquities, whose importance had been barely considered before 1851, now moved from a cramped upper western gallery into the upper southern range.

A certain amount of desperation appears to have informed the Treasury's attitude as, with the departure of natural history, the Museum still wailed that it needed more space. However difficult the Treasury may have been, it must be remembered that it had to balance competing demands on the national purse and over the years it had provided very large sums. A Special Committee, including a Treasury delegate, was appointed in February 1885 to 'consider suggestions made by the Lords Commissioners of the Treasury for reducing or restricting the growth of the Museum collections' and a report was issued in May. This was not a meeting of minds and the Treasury can only have despaired on reading the Keeper of Greek and Roman Antiquities' defence of the extensive display of Greek vases:

> The vases . . . of dates covering a period of many centuries . . . are of almost infinite variety of forms . . . For the satisfaction of ordinary visitors an excellent exhibition of these beautiful objects could be compressed into a moderate space; – but for purposes of studious research to work out problems of ancient art none of them are superfluous.

The Trustees reminded the Treasury that the collection of antiquities had been formed largely by donations on the understanding that these objects would not be disposed of. And also – 'it is quite beyond the power of the Trustees, if it were their desire, to prevent the further discovery of buried statues and friezes.' But, more importantly, they pointed out a truth often forgotten:

> . . . it is apparent that the idea prevails that the Museum may be treated, in respect to the Antiquities, as a place of exhibition of objects designed to interest the general visitor. Your Committee, however, consider it most important that the collections should be formed with the view to afford to students the means of prosecuting their researches, since on these the public at large are mainly dependent for the instruction to be derived from the Antiquities exhibited.

THE WHITE WING

Some of the pressure for space was lessened by an unexpected legacy from a certain William White (1800-23). The Trustees could only conjecture that, as he had lived in the vicinity – in Store Street and later in Tavistock Square – he had decided to do something about the appalling lack of space available in 1822 (when his will was made). His land and other property were left first to his wife (provided she did not remarry) with an interest in the land only to his infant son, then to the Museum. Setting out his wishes regarding his legacy to the Museum, White wrote that:

> The money and property so bequeathed to the British Museum I wish to be employed in building or improving upon the said Institution, and that round the Frieze of some part of such Building, or, if this money is otherwise employed, then over or upon that which has so employed it, the words 'Gulielmus White Arm. Brittannica dicavit 18...' be carved, or words to that import: it is a little vanity of no harm and may tempt others to follow my example, in thinking more of the Nation and less of themselves.

White's son died young, but Mrs White survived for a further fifty-six years, dying in 1879. The Principal Librarian noted that Mrs White's brother, then 91, was probably alone in retaining a personal recollection of White, whom he described as 'highly intelligent, with scientific tastes, and fond of art'. The legacy amounted to £71,780 – a handsome sum, sufficient for a building. The Trustees tried to avoid legacy duty but the Treasury insisted on its £6,369 slice.

As early as 1848 Sydney Smirke had been asked to prepare rough costings for the erection of a building in open space along the west side of Montague Street. In 1861 he had produced a plan for a building in the garden of the Principal Librarian's residence. Various proposals were put forward for the use of this space, one persistent one being that the building should house the Trustees' boardroom, Principal Librarian's and Secretary's offices transferred from the west, thereby allowing the southward extension of the Egyptian Sculpture Gallery. The White bequest now meant that the building could be more extensive than anything the Treasury was inclined to fund, while at the same time the Treasury's refusal of funding for a proposed building south of the Lycian Gallery meant that the Boardroom and offices might as well stay where they were. Also, since the Treasury was prepared to fund an extension linking the Elgin Room to the space occupied by the Print and Insect Rooms (pp. 26-8), some additional space for classical sculpture was in any case available. The 1862 plan had envisaged that the new building would provide space for the Departments of Prints and Drawings and Coins and Medals. It was subsequently decided to put Coin and Medals over the Archaic Room (pp. 34-5). This left Prints and Drawings still looking for a new home, while the space not now used by the other departments could be allocated to Newspapers, Oriental Printed Books and Manuscripts.

The earlier Smirke plan was revived by the Trustees, who handed it over to the Surveyor of the Office of Works, Sir John Taylor. Taylor, who in later years was responsible for, amongst other buildings, the War Office in Whitehall, the Chancery Lane front of the Public Record Office and the main staircase and central rooms of the National Gallery, kept to Smirke's Greek Revival style.

The estimated cost of the new building left a surplus of some £13,000 which the Trustees decided to use for a new Mausoleum Room (p. 55, the area now occupied by the Architecture and Hellenistic Rooms), a new boiler house and the transfer of bindery staff displaced by the White Wing.

In September 1882 the cornerstone of the White Wing was laid by the Principal Librarian, Edward Bond. In February 1883 the Trustees received a gentle reminder from Taylor that Surveyors of the Office of Works were allowed to receive a small commission or a gratuity for acting as architects for considerable public works, and a payment of 1 per cent would be appreciated. The final payment under contract was made in January 1884. Sir Edward Bond was still in residence, although it cannot have been much fun living next door to a building site. He was obliged to install stained glass in the window of his sitting room, which immediately overlooked the new building.

33. *This unusual photograph of the Museum from the south-east was taken c. 1900. It shows the East Residences in the foreground. The door facing the front railing was to Sydney Colvin's residence (Keeper of Prints and Drawings) and to the right Edward J. L. Scott's residence (Keeper of Manuscripts). Beyond is Sir John Taylor's White Wing surrounded by the remains of the Principal Librarian's garden.*

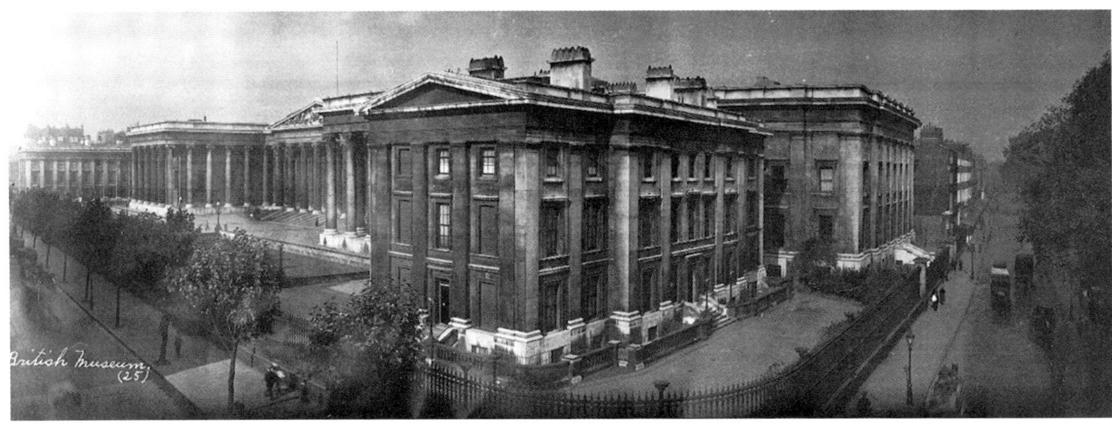

During 1884–5 lifts and central heating were installed. The Trustees authorized the supply of the new electric light (p.56) to readers' rooms and staff studies, although, since this was beyond the capacity of the Siemens steam engine, lights elsewhere in the Museum were withdrawn. The Trustees were less sympathetic about the telephone, however, and insisted that speaking tubes up to 700 feet (213 m) long would be adequate. The wing eventually cost £48,970.

The Trustees may to some extent have obtained their revenge for the Treasury's taking a slice of White's bequest. In 1885 their request for £10,410 for fittings in the new building was met by a Treasury letter 'expressing surprise that the cost of furnishing the building is thrown upon the Parliamentary vote'.

Prints and Drawings moved into the mezzanine floor on the east front in 1885, but it proved to be badly lit and in 1887 the Print Room was transferred to the upper north level, with exhibitions located on the upper eastern floor and their offices in the mezzanine below. In 1888 an exhibition of glass and ceramics given by A.W. Franks opened in the upper southern section. On the ground floor were for the first time Manuscripts' and Newspapers' students' rooms.

The White Wing is relatively unaltered, although changes have been made in the use of the space.

The Mausoleum Room

The surplus from White's bequest was used to provide proper accommodation for the Mausoleum sculptures from Halicarnassus, which at one time had been languishing on the colonnade. The new gallery was constructed between 1881 and October 1882 in the open space parallel with the main western gallery. It opened to the public in 1884. This being a generous bequest, some of the money was spent on a splendid mosaic floor consisting of a border surrounding an area of white, in preference to the more usual York stone.

This no longer exists in its original state, a mezzanine having been inserted in the 1960s and a public lecture theatre constructed in part of the lower level. The upper level was refurbished as the Hellenistic Gallery in 1995, the southern entrance of which reverted to a style more in keeping with Smirke's original designs.

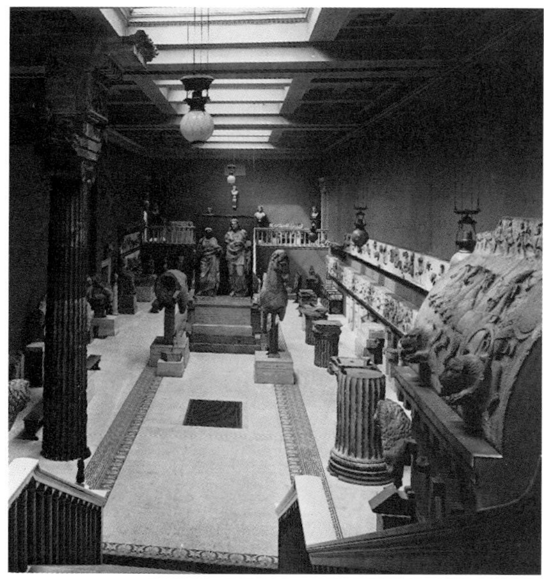

34. *Photograph by Donald Macbeth of the Mausoleum Room in 1908, a quarter of a century after construction, showing its mosaic floor and improvements to the electric lighting. One of the Stevens lions (see p.40 and title page) may be glimpsed at the foot of the staircase (on the left).*

White's money also provided for the construction of a brick-built bindery in the north-west corner of the site, which still survives.

The second Phigaleian Room

Once Prints and Drawings were settled in the White Wing it was possible for the middle floor of this gallery in the north-west corner to be remodelled, the insects having gone to South Kensington. The ground floor was raised to the level of the Elgin Gallery, skylights introduced into the roof and the windows blocked. A door was constructed from the Elgin Gallery (now the Nereid Room). In 1889 the Phigaleian marbles were rearranged here.

Today the only trace of the Insect Room is a row of bricked-up windows outside. This room now contains the Payava tomb and the Caryatid from the Erechtheion. It was much altered in the 1960s remodelling.

ELECTRIC LIGHT

A full understanding of the Museum's early buildings has to take into account the Trustees' acute horror of fire, for, unlike in other premises, naked flames were forbidden. Lanterns were permitted but, certainly by the mid-nineteenth century, they were only provided lit and locked, the key being held by a responsible person outside the main building. The Townley Gallery and Sir Robert Smirke's building were therefore designed to take advantage of direct and borrowed natural daylight. However, when it got dark and on smog-filled days the Museum closed.

Gas, too, was considered unsafe for the artificial illumination of the galleries. Nevertheless, it was used for the lamps in the forecourt in 1818 and then quietly carried into some staff residences. This came as something of an unpleasant surprise to the Trustees in 1847, when the Keeper of Antiquities made the mistake of asking official permission for gas to be installed in his new Smirke-designed residence, the Keeper of Zoology having already done so. The Trustees, appalled to find that gas was already a *fait accompli*, hurriedly issued instructions that it was not to be installed in future in any Museum building or residence without their express permission. Fittings for gas lighting were put into the new Reading Room but they were never used, and in 1866 the Trustees at last approved the use of gas in the residences.

For these reasons the Museum was one of the pioneers in the use of electricity for lighting public buildings. In December 1878 the Principal Librarian was given permission to approach the Office of Works for advice and assistance. There was a bewildering range of systems available but the Société Général d'Electricité was willing to try a free experiment with the 'Jablochkoff candle', a type of carbon arc lamp. Power was provided by steam engine and dynamo. On 24 February 1879 there was an unusual occurrence – a murmur of spontaneous applause from readers as the Reading Room was lit for the first time. *The Times* recorded the events of a foggy morning: 'shortly after 10 o'clock when many readers unmindful of the improvements of the age were about to quit with their papers, the electric light was turned on, and, without any apparent preparations the spacious room was suddenly illuminated as by a magic ray of sunshine.'

In the winter of 1879/80 the Trustees introduced the cheaper Siemens system. Like the Jablochkoff candle, the first lamps were open, with a disconcerting habit of discarding carbon on anything below them. In February 1880, after a piece of carbon nearly ignited some papers and with them the Reading Room, closed lamps were substituted. A great advance was the invention of the Swan lamp, a small incandescent globe made to contain a filament within a vacuum. These were rather expensive – 25*s*. each – but were introduced into the readers' lavatories in 1881, from which two were accordingly stolen. The Trustees took the only practical course to stop the unknown thief and had the lamps raised out of readers' reach.

Initially the Trustees hired the system for the winter and discontinued it during the summer months. From the Reading Room and Hall the electric light began to spread, but the Treasury was reluctant to sanction the capital expenditure for a full system. However, against a background of Parliamentary agitation for evening opening of museums in the winter months, it acquiesced in 1889. On 28 January 1890 the entire Museum was at last lit by electricity. A private view was held, to which 3,000 were invited. For the Victorians the new illumination was a revelation. Sculptures hidden for generations in dark corners were now properly visible.

The Museum generated its own electricity until 1935 when it was provided by a local supply company.

THE MEDAL ROOM

In the new Smirke building the Department of Coins and Medals was located next to the Gold Ornament Room at the upper southern end of the West Wing. In May 1879 the Keeper first urged on the Principal Librarian the need for a new Medal Room above the Lycian Gallery (by then the Archaic Room, pp. 34–5). In 1882 the Trustees asked for plans to be prepared. By October 1883 the Department was becoming desperate: 'owing to the rapid increase of the collections of coins and medals the present Department has become a mere store-room, it being necessary to pile up the cabinets upon the floor of the Medal Room and upon the bar intended for the use of students.' By 1887 a quarter of the bar had been occupied by the creeping coin cabinets; by 1888 sixty cabinets were piled up on the floor. In 1890 funds were at last granted by the Treasury. The new floor above the Archaic Room was completed at the end of 1892 and the removal of the quarter of a million specimens (460 cabinets, 12,500 trays) was effected by February 1893.

The Medal Room was completely destroyed during the air raid of 10/11 May 1941 (p. 65; the collections had been removed to the country in 1939) but was rebuilt and reopened in 1959. A desperate need for space was met in the 1980s when a mezzanine floor was inserted in the ceiling of what had been the Archaic (previously Lycian) Room.

THE BM 'ISLAND'

Towards the end of the nineteenth century (with an eye on the twentieth) the Trustees purchased the sixty-nine surrounding houses and 5½ acres of land (on Montague Place, Bedford Square, Bloomsbury Street, Great Russell Street, and Montague Street) from the Bedford Estates 'for the gradual extension and enlargement of the British Museum as when occasion may arise and circumstance may permit'.

The thought had previously occurred to the Trustees in 1848 and 1857. At the time the proposal was put to the Treasury in 1894 there was a *fin de siècle* gloom, a letter pointing out: 'The present is, to say the least, an unpropitious moment for the proposal. The Revenue of the country is not thriving, the demands on the Exchequer are unprecedentally large, and it is impossible to ask Parliament to vote this immense sum as part of the yearly expenditure of the State.' The Trustees were, however, offered, somewhat grudgingly, a loan of £200,000, repayment to be made over a period of fifty years. The arrangements for the purchase from the Bedford Estates were completed in 1895.

The houses on the northern side were demolished for the construction of King Edward VII's Galleries (pp. 59-60). The others are now protected but the Museum retains the freeholds.

THE NEWSPAPER LIBRARY

A newspaper storage building (the 'Hendon Repository') was constructed at Colindale in North London between 1904 and 1905. Fitting out and removal of the collections took until 1906. Readers continued to use the ground floor of the White Wing until the Newspaper Library, with a reading room, opened at Colindale in 1932.

THE BURNET SCHEME

Land for expansion now being available, the possibility of a new building first became a practicable proposition when in 1899 a bequest of £50,000 (£45,000 after the Treasury's slice of legacy duty) was received from Vincent Stuckey Lean (1820-99) The terms of the bequest were that the sum left to the Trustees should 'be appropriated at their discretion to the improvement and extension of the Library and Reading Room'. Lean was another unexpected donor. Born in Bristol, he worked briefly in Stuckey's Bank and then was called to the Bar in 1843. He spent some time abroad and abandoned his Bar career in 1854, devoting his life to researching the proverbs of all nations. Unmarried, he dined frequently at the Inner Temple and a Memoir states that:

> On giving up his Chambers, he never again settled into rooms of his own, though always intending to do so. His books and other property were packed in cases and stored away in London from 1855 and after . . . His life was of the simplest and most self-denying; after an early breakfast came the reading at the British Museum; then to the Windham Club for mid-day meal, papers, etc.

The Lean bequest being insufficient, an application for additional funds was put to the Treasury, which, concerned at the financial situation because of the Boer War, insisted that the Museum reduce its collections. A Bill was introduced into Parliament but withdrawn following strenuous opposition. In 1903, however, £150,000 was offered – with strings attached, for the Treasury and the Office of Works largely controlled the project. Early that year general plans were sketched out by the Office of Works (Mr Tanner) in the style of the White Wing, but in 1904 these were scrapped.

In May 1904 Aston Webb, President of the Royal Institute of British Architects, wrote to Sir Schomberg McDonnell of the Office of Works with a list nominated by the RIBA Council of seven architects 'of taste, skill, and efficiency in Classical design who would in their opinion be the best qualified to carry out the proposed additions to the British Museum.' John James Burnet was selected in 1905. The son of a successful Glasgow architect, Burnet spent three years in Paris during the late 1870s studying engineering as well as architecture, followed by a study tour of France and Italy. On his return to Glasgow he worked on the designs for the Royal Institute for Fine Arts, Glasgow (1881), the offices of the Clyde Navigation Trust (1886) and the Glasgow Athenaeum (1889), all in the 'Neo-Grecian' style. By 1890 he was experimenting with the Gothic style, first seen in his design for the Barony Church, Glasgow.

The commission for the design of the new Museum buildings was intended to be the first stage of a well-conceived scheme to spread out on all four sides. Monumental galleries would flatten the surrounding buildings; a domed lecture theatre would be erected off Bedford Square. There would be no more calls for extra space (at least not for a while)! The proposals were in essence part of a major renaissance for Bloomsbury and Holborn. A vast area to the east of the Museum, comprising mainly squalid, cramped dwellings and small shops, was swept away around 1900 to make way for new roads and municipal and commercial buildings. Kingsway and Aldwych, grand thoroughfares of

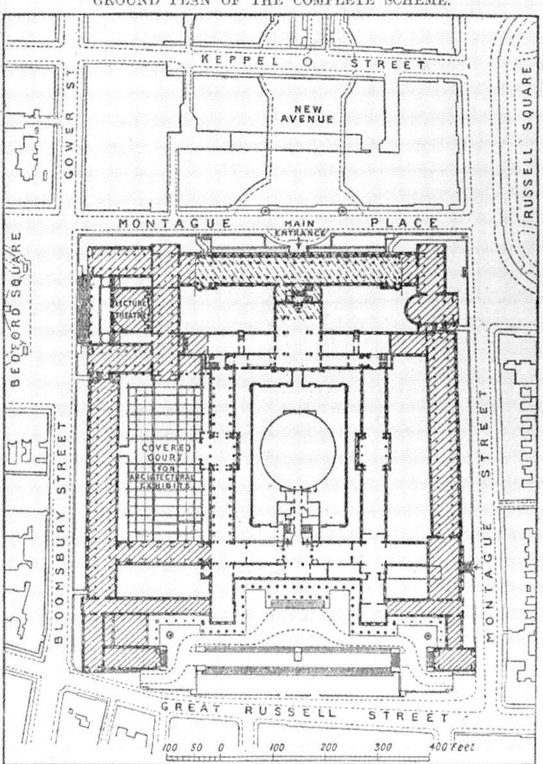

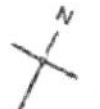

36. *The proposed expansion of the Museum site was debated by the press during 1907 and was favourably received. As well as King Edward VII's Galleries and the ill-fated additional wings proposed by Burnet, the scheme included a grand avenue to the north and a 'Covered Court for Architectural Exhibits'. Thirty years later the latter area, on the west of the Museum site, was the scene of much activity with the building of the Duveen Gallery. (Plan from* The Times, *21 January 1911.)*

35. *Burnet's model (c.1910) of King Edward VII's Galleries. The iron railings (lost to war salvage) and the Frampton lions are visible, as are the proposed additional sculptures which were never commissioned.*

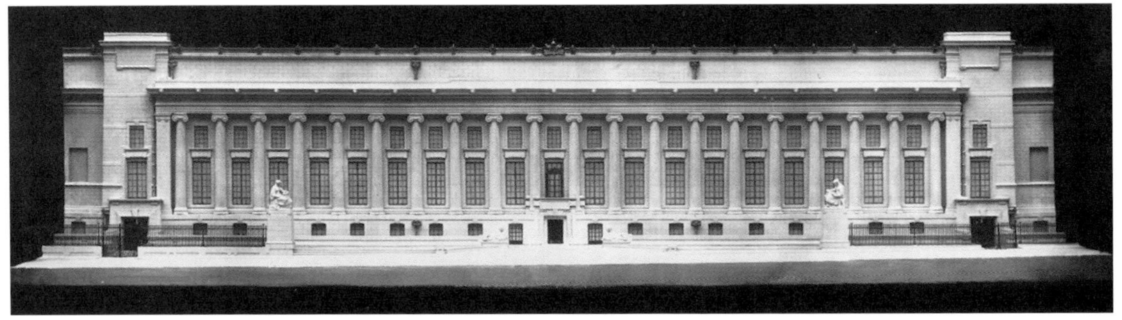

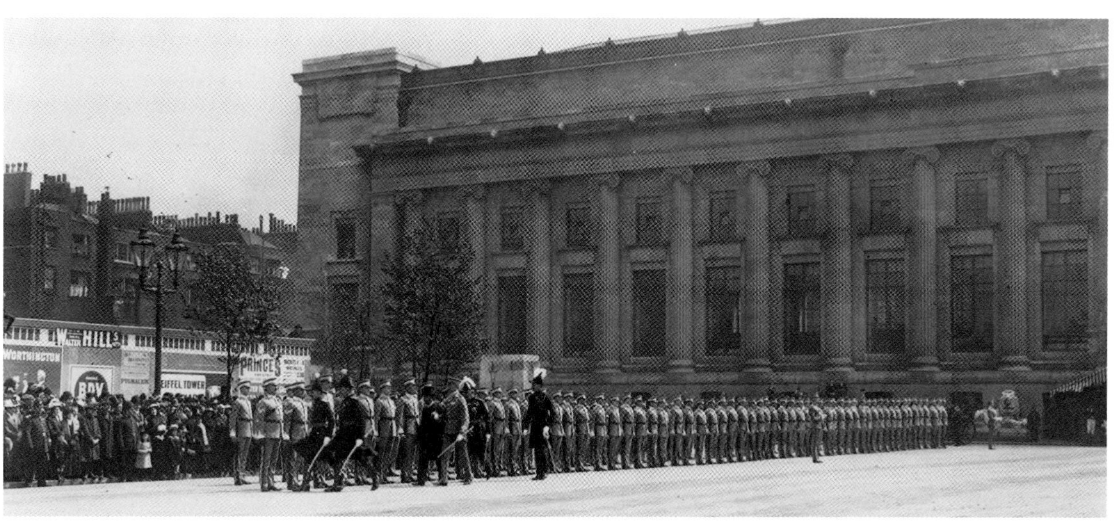

37. *The opening of King Edward VII's Galleries on 7 May 1914 by King George V and Queen Mary. The guard was formed by the Brigade of the Artists' Rifles and the opening ceremony took place in the North Library.*

some 100 feet (30.5 m) wide, were constructed by 1905 and Burnet was responsible for two of the most impressive buildings, the new offices of the General Accident, Fire, and Life Assurance Corporation in Aldwych, and the premises of the Kodak Company in Kingsway.

KING EDWARD VII'S GALLERIES

Burnet's plans for the first stage of the project – a building to the north of the Museum – were approved by the Trustees in December 1904, and in April 1906 the first contract for the building of the basement and sub-ground floors was entered into. The relationship with the Office of Works, behind whom was the Treasury, was not a happy one and the Trustees subsequently recorded:

> ... that, with a regrettable lack of official courtesy, HM Office of Works have never informed the Trustees of the commencement of building operations or completion of contracts. The mere fact of workmen being admitted to the premises, and the obtaining of information from independent sources, have been the only means by which the Trustees could guess that work was being undertaken on their own premises.

In April 1907 the Office of Works arbitrarily announced that the estimate for engineering services was now £25,000, double the original £13,000 estimate. This meant less money available for the building proper. The Trustees fumed but got nowhere.

On 27 June 1907 the foundation stone (now above the entrance) was laid by King Edward VII. The King, who had been an active Museum Trustee for twenty years prior to his accession, agreed that the new building might bear his name.

Not everything went smoothly at the formal ceremony. The *Star* recorded that:

> The brilliance of the spectacle at the British Museum this afternoon, when King Edward – who was accompanied by Queen Alexandra – laid the foundation-stone of the new wing, was marred by the absence of the Mayor of Holborn and his satellites.
>
> ... The truth is that the Mayor and Aldermen of the borough of Holborn have been snubbed... It should be understood that his Worship the Mayor . . . received invitation cards to attend today's function ... for two seats in Row 6, Block B. Thinking there was some mistake the Mayor instructed the Town Clerk to write a dignified letter to the authorities. Could it be that some underling in a Government office was deliberately ignoring the majesty of the rulers of the borough in which the Museum stands?
>
> It could.

> The polite official answer was to the effect that the authorities could not make any alteration in the arrangements.
>
> Then it was that the Mayor of the Borough where the scandals came from asserted his dignity. He sent his ticket and the Town Clerk's ticket back . . .
>
> And it is almost with regret we have to record that the stone-laying went off without a hitch . . . the new wing . . . will stand for ever as a memorial of the day when the Mayor and Corporation of Holborn asserted their dignity.

Perhaps the Mayor did not forgive this snub too easily, since in 1912, the Borough having promised to re-lay the Montague Place roadway at a level compatible with the new building, Holborn workmen were observed resurfacing it at the original level (p.77).

Behind the scenes there was more trouble. Eighteen months after the foundation stone was laid no progress whatever had been made on the main structure. Work was resumed early in 1910 when the contract for the main building was given to W. E. Blake of Plymouth. By the beginning of 1911 the main external structure was almost completed and plans for the internal furniture and fittings had been prepared. Although it had been hoped that the building would be handed over by the contractor in the course of 1912, there was a further delay and the handover by the First Commissioner of Works did not take place until October 1913. By the end of the year the transfer of the collections had begun. The building was formally opened on 7 May 1914 by King George V and Queen Mary.

The building, described by Pevsner (1948) as being 'in the chastest Beaux Arts style', is embellished with twenty engaged Ionic columns similar to those of the main front of the Museum but raised 14 feet (4.3 m) above street level. The façade, of Portland stone, is flanked by two massive towers or 'pylons' 90 feet (27.4 m) high. The outer walls and pedestals of the forecourt are of Scottish granite. The two limestone lions flanking the entrance are by Sir George Frampton (1860-1928). The Museum could not at first afford them, due to the Treasury arbitrarily deciding that they were not worth the £2,000 agreed with the sculptor and halving the money available. They could, after all, said the Treasury, be left 'in the rough'. This provoked an anguished letter from the Trustees:

> Such a course they believe would expose all concerned to ridicule; and . . . , in all probability, having regard to the common tendency of temporary expedients to become permanent, the lions would remain rough-hewn for all time – monuments of unhappy differences of opinion among their creators, a puzzle to the 'studious and curious' on whose behalf the British Museum was founded, and a source of contention among students of natural history.

The matter was resolved by Frampton agreeing to reduce his price. Other statues – of Art and Science – had been intended for the building but were never executed.

The *Builder's* reaction to the façade was mixed:

> The exterior view of the new wing is, on the whole, satisfactory enough, but the heavy railings which can be passed at either side of the entrance are too elaborate for a sham defence, and the repetition of 'E.R.', and a crown on the cornice is singularly ineffective, while the beauty of the leadwork is lost, and when seen is not wholly appropriate. It is also unfortunate that the mistake committed in the old buildings is repeated here, and the external walls not faced with stone upon the inner side, probably because those walls are not supposed to show.

Burnet was knighted on the completion of the building and received a number of architectural honours. His *DNB* entry, perhaps a little prematurely, singles out King Edward VII's Galleries as 'one of the most important contributions to the architecture of this century . . . justly acclaimed for its modern vigour and originality'.

The First World War broke out in August 1914. Transfer of the collections to the new galleries had already been delayed by a dispute in the building trade in the early months of 1914; then in 1916, in the interests of economy, the Government ordered the closure of museums and galleries in London. An attempt by the Air Board to take over the premises, thereby making the Museum building a tempting target, was successfully fought off. Installing exhibitions in the new galleries was halted when parts of the building were temporarily handed over to other government departments.

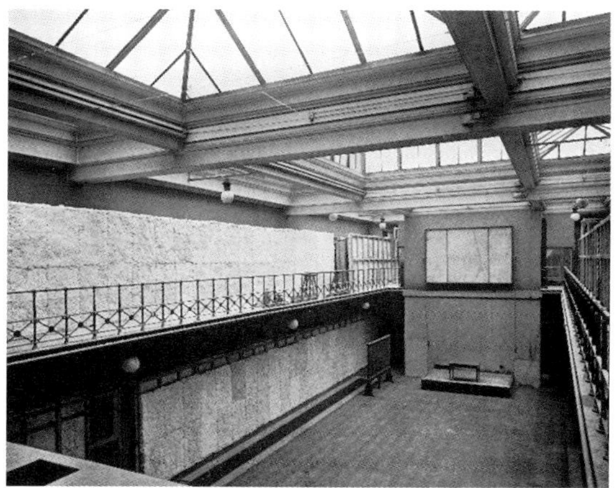

38. *Collections too large for evacuation during the First World War were protected* in situ. *Here, in 1917, sculptured slabs in the Assyrian Basement (one of the additional galleries designed by Sir John Taylor) are being boxed. Commonly called the 'Swimming Pool', this gallery survived until the early 1960s.*

Because of the danger of bombing, some of the collections were removed out of London, to a nearby Post Office tunnel or to specially reinforced basements. Some of the larger objects elsewhere in the Museum were sandbagged *in situ*, forming a somewhat surrealistic display inaccessible to the public.

It was not until the 1920s that the building was free of its unwanted tenants. The Prints and Drawings students' room, gallery and storage occupied the top floor, with offices below for that department and also Maps and Music and library departments on the ground floor.

The main gallery, which contained the medieval collections and European pottery and porcelain in the western section and oriental ceramics and glass in the eastern, opened in 1920-21. At the extreme west end, containing the greater part of the Franks Bequest, was the Franks Room which opened in 1923. At the east end the Waddesdon collection was displayed in specially constructed elaborately carved exhibition cases, some of which still survive.

A temporary corridor was built connecting the north-east staircase of the old building at the north end of the King's Library to the ground-floor gallery pending the construction of the next phase of Burnet's scheme. This eventually opened in

39. *One hundred and fifty mahogany storage presses were removed from the old Prints and Drawings accommodation in the White Wing to the new students' room on the top floor of King Edward VII's Galleries. During the winter of 1913/14 a team of carpenters set about re-siting the old presses and constructing new presses to match the originals.*

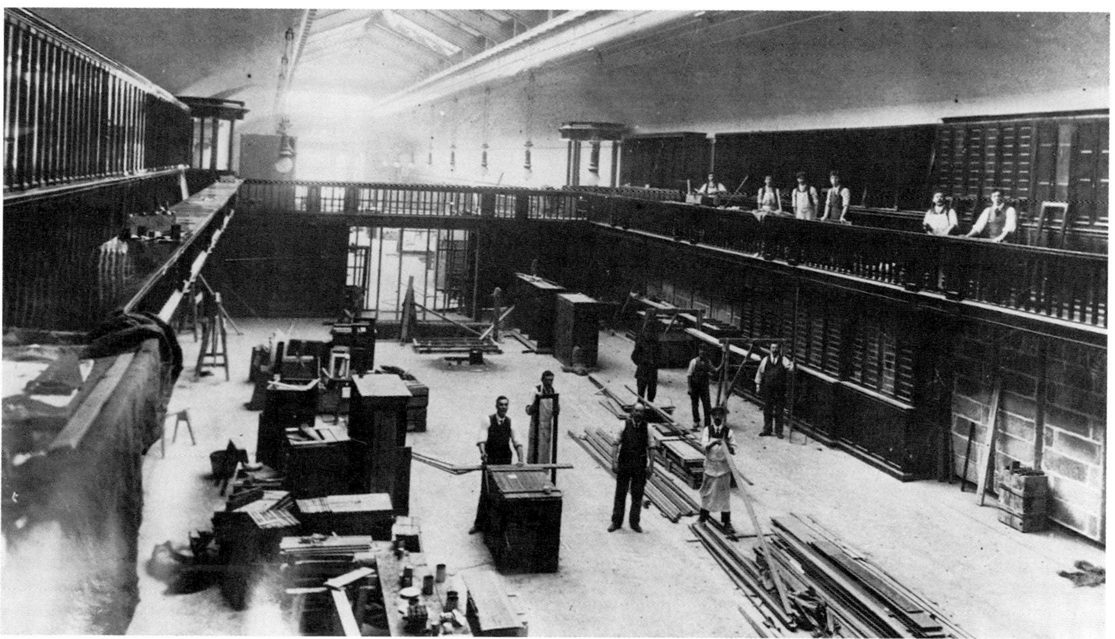

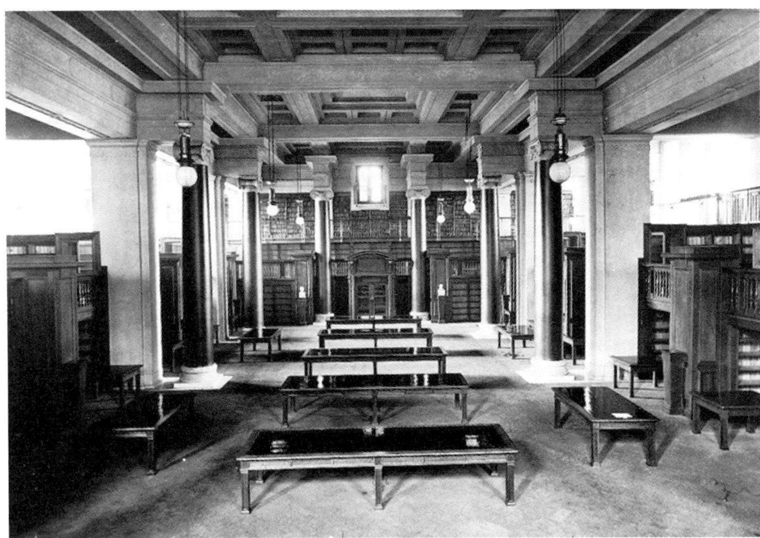

40. *Burnet's North Library soon after the official opening in May 1914. Twenty-two years later this fine room was remodelled.*

1922. The imposing North Entrance did not open to the public until 1931, and then only briefly because of lack of funds to staff it. The main route therefore was from the centre of the upper northern galleries.

The North Library

One of the lost rooms of the Museum is Burnet's North Library, although it would appear that contemporary views of its quality varied. *The Times* on 11 November 1913 noted that it was one of the most important rooms in the new building (see col. pl. 6). However, the *Builder* was less keen: 'The new Large Room is, frankly, not wholly a success. It is dark, massive, full of woodwork, and the painted pillars at one end are unsatisfactory in material and position alike.' This was a loftier extension of the old 'Large Room' (p. 25). The walls took two galleries of books: the lower of these was wide, with bays, and under it ran a service passage, diverting the traffic that used to pass through the Large Room. A deeply elaborate coffered ceiling and pairs of square white stone and round black columns standing forward of the gallery along the sides of the room added to its architectural dignity, while the columns reduced the span of the girders carrying the floor above.

The uses of King Edward VII's Galleries have changed over time. The mezzanine still houses offices, but the western side is designated for the Korean Gallery on the departure of Maps and Music. The western side of the floor above, now Oriental and Prints and Drawings exhibitions, was much altered during 1970-71 and also during the construction of the Japanese Galleries (p.69), although Burnet's Print Room remains. The railings outside were removed for scrap during the Second World War.

In 1912, with the first phase of Burnet's Museum scheme almost finished, W. R. Lethaby produced an equally visionary scheme to link the Museum and Waterloo Bridge by an impressive avenue which would have complemented the proposed King George V Avenue which led northwards from the new galleries. Lethaby's ideas were not realized and Burnet's avenue survived incomplete for twenty years, until it was irrevocably blocked by the purchase of land to the north of the Museum by the University of London in 1927 and the construction of Senate House in 1934-5. For Burnet it must have been a double blow, as his monumental 1907 and 1918 proposals for the new Selfridge department store in Oxford Street (which would not have been out of place within his Bloomsbury scheme) did not materialize. The accolade of an RIBA Gold Medal in 1923 was almost spoiled by anxious Museum Trustees poised for a legal confrontation. Corroding beams and inferior reinforced concrete had been discovered in King Edward VII's Galleries. In 1926, confronted with a hefty bill for repairs, the Trustees took legal advice and looked to the architect for compensation. Fortunately for all concerned, at the last moment they reconsidered their position and withdrew.

BETWEEN THE WARS – MEZZANINES AND BOOKSTACKS

The inter-war years were not a propitious time for development. In October 1919, yet again in desperate need of space, the Trustees approved a plan put forward by the Office of Works to add a new storey on the Iron Library (the bookstacks surrounding the Reading Room). Alterations were carried out on the south-east section in 1923 but funds were not immediately available for further work. In May 1926, doubts having been expressed as to the ability of the structure to withstand an extra floor, a survey concluded that while the Reading Room was structurally sound, the Iron Library was structurally inadequate and could not bear the weight. A 1929 report by the Royal Commission on National Museums and Galleries recommended the replacement of the four library quadrant bookstacks. The north-west was replaced in 1934; the north-east was structurally complete but lacked shelves when war broke out in 1939. The south-west was demolished by the Luftwaffe in 1941 and rebuilt after the war (completed in 1954).

41. *This photograph, taken from the Fifth Egyptian Gallery in 1932, shows the old Catalogue Room (originally the Reading Room of 1838-57). The cast iron beams, stamped John Bradley, Stourbridge, 1834, were replaced by steel girders during the construction of the North Wing mezzanines. The area below window level is now the Mexican Gallery.*

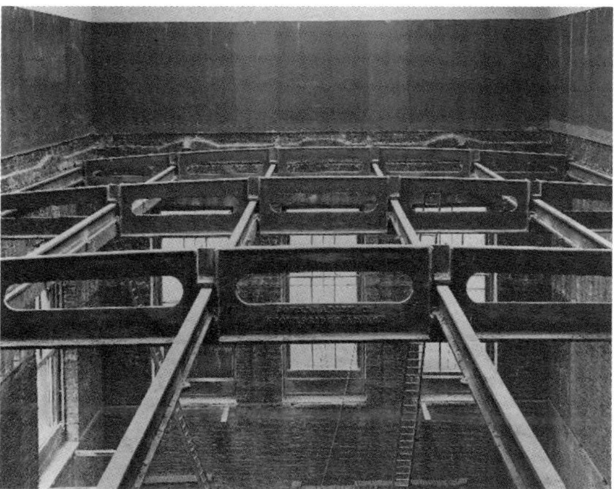

The Royal Commission had also recommended the construction of additional floors in the 'Supplementary Rooms' to the west of the North Library. In July 1932 the Trustees discussed a report compiled by the National Physical Laboratory on the strength of cast iron girders supporting certain galleries on the upper floor. Rather alarmingly, the Office of Works subsequently recommended the closure of the Fourth and Fifth Egyptian galleries and the Babylonian Room and required that the number of visitors to other upper galleries be regulated (there ensued a period of intensive visitor counting). The replacement of defective iron beams in the North Wing did, however, present the opportunity to introduce these mezzanine floors to increase accommodation, creating a labyrinth in which rooms east and west, north and south do not necessarily match and are not necessarily on exactly the same level. In 1932 the Trustees decided that in all future reconstruction mezzanine floors should be inserted where the architectural conditions allowed. To provide access to the new floors the east and west staircases were replaced.

On 14 October 1933 the Office of Works and the Treasury approved the construction of a mezzanine over Burnet's North Library to provide office and storage space for Egyptian and Assyrian Antiquities. The Office of Works had been opposed to the inclusion of the North Library in the mezzanine building scheme as this would destroy Burnet's impressive room. The library's fate was sealed, however, when it was found that Burnet had created a void ten feet (3 m) in height between the coffered ceiling and the floor above. This was a serious fire risk and a waste of valuable space.

The designer was John Markham, working to the Chief Architect of the Office of Works. On 13 July 1935 the Trustees considered a sketch and noted that, owing to the insertion of the mezzanine floor, the room would not admit of conventional architectural treatment, being too low and dark for its purpose. They preferred that the supports should not be disguised with round columns but enclosed in sheet lining of the same square plan. They also disapproved of concealed lighting at the tops of the columns and preferred some system of undisguised lighting. Various methods were

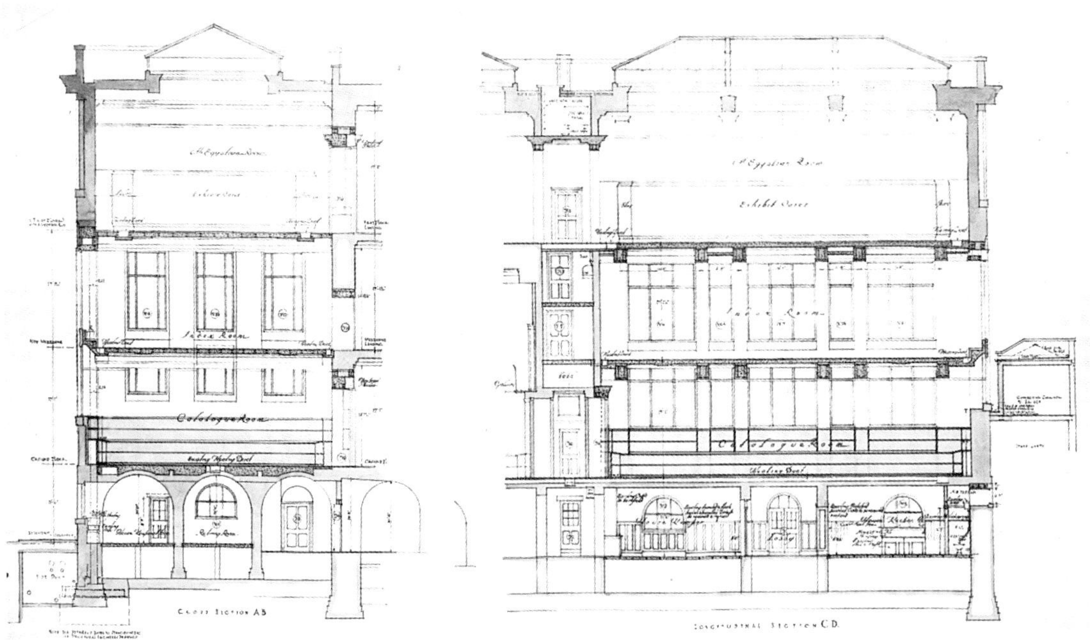

42. *Sectional drawings showing alterations to the Catalogue Room and the new mezzanine floor (Index Room) in the North Wing, July 1932. Robert Smirke's windows were removed during this reconstruction. The wing's 'Great Court' façade will be restored to its original neo-classical splendour.*

devised to visually enlarge and lighten the area. The architect referred to the peculiar difficulties that 'this problem presents . . . the unalterable elements in the problem are such as to almost cause despair'. Markham was obliged to provide a full size mock-up of a column and wrote:

> After hearing my explanations the Trustees accept the circular cylindrical column, with fluted surfaces, but express a preference for a cap which finishes tight up to the ceiling instead of having a metal dish finish below ceiling level as I had proposed. . . . [the Trustees'] suggestions, if adopted, would reduce the whole thing to a most commonplace level.

The reconstruction began in 1936 and the North Library reopened to readers on 25 October 1937.

Only the shell of the North Library remains. This will become an Ethnography gallery.

THE DUVEEN GALLERY

In 1928 the Museum acquired its first living private benefactor for the building. A report of the Royal Commission on National Museums and Galleries had commented adversely on the overcrowded conditions in which the Parthenon sculptures were then displayed. This elicited an offer from the dealer Sir Joseph Duveen to build a new gallery for the sculptures at his expense. He insisted on appointing the architect and in 1930 John Russell Pope, who designed the Jefferson Memorial and the National Gallery of Art, Washington, was invited to draw up plans. In 1931 a formal agreement was concluded between Duveen and the Office of Works by which Sir Joseph agreed to provide £150,000 for the new gallery and also for the Nereid monument.

The then Museum Secretary recalled that:

> . . . benefactors are kittle cattle to shoo behind and Joe Duveen was not less so than others. With fine artistic taste, he had little knowledge of archaeology . . . Duveen . . . had a curious, machine-gun-like and hypnotising way of talking, assuming your agreement with what he was saying, which needed real knowledge to stand up to . . . But he

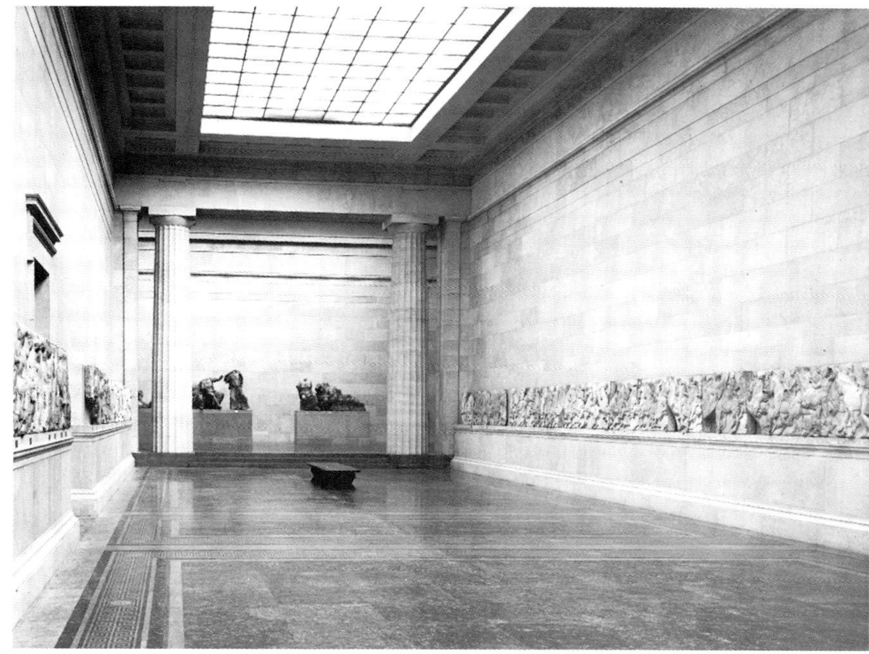

43. *The Duveen Gallery, completed in 1939, on the day of its opening, 18 June 1962 – a delay of twenty-three years. (After the war the sculptures were temporarily displayed in the old Elgin Room.)*

> was a generous and friendly man . . . and in the end the Museum got a new Elgin Room to be proud of.

In July 1933 the Trustees took over the leases of their properties in Bedford Square backing on to the Museum so that work could start, but a Mr Eden in No. 2 had his fifteen minutes, or rather three years, of fame, delaying the project until mid-1936 when he refused to allow work to begin until the ending of his lease, in spite of all Duveen's entreaties. This was to have unfortunate results since the building was only completed at the beginning of 1939. Time required for the installation of the sculptures and a formal opening ran out with the declaration of war in September of that year. The sculptures were removed for safety.

The walls of the Duveen Gallery are gris d'Alesia (a French limestone) and the floor black marble (Nero Nube) from a quarry near Avrisina, Trieste. A new seam of the marble had to be opened for the gallery's post-war restoration.

The gallery was damaged in 1940. Restoration and the addition of an electrostatic precipitator for cleansing the air began in 1960 and the gallery was opened by the Archbishop of Canterbury on 18 June 1962. There have been subsequent improvements and the two parallel narrow galleries now house an introductory display. The basements under the Duveen Gallery were remodelled as the Wolfson Galleries of Classical Sculpture and Inscriptions and opened in 1985.

THE SECOND WORLD WAR AND ITS AFTERMATH

It has been calculated that during the Second World War in the area of London in which the British Museum is situated there was an average of two high-explosive bombs to every three acres, exclusive of incendiaries, flying bombs and mines. The Museum had seven high-explosive bombs – slightly under its fair share of eight. Two in September 1940 came through the same hole in King Edward VII's Galleries four days apart, both failing to explode. Part of the ceiling and much of the plasterwork of a section of the King's Library were also damaged. In October 1940 the dome of the Round Reading Room was seen to be burning and flickering 'like a Christmas pudding', but fortunately the interior did not ignite. The Newspaper Library at Colindale was badly damaged and the Duveen Gallery was hit.

On the night of 10/11 May 1941 700 tons of bombs were dropped on London, starting 2,200 fires. The Museum's luck ran out when a stick of

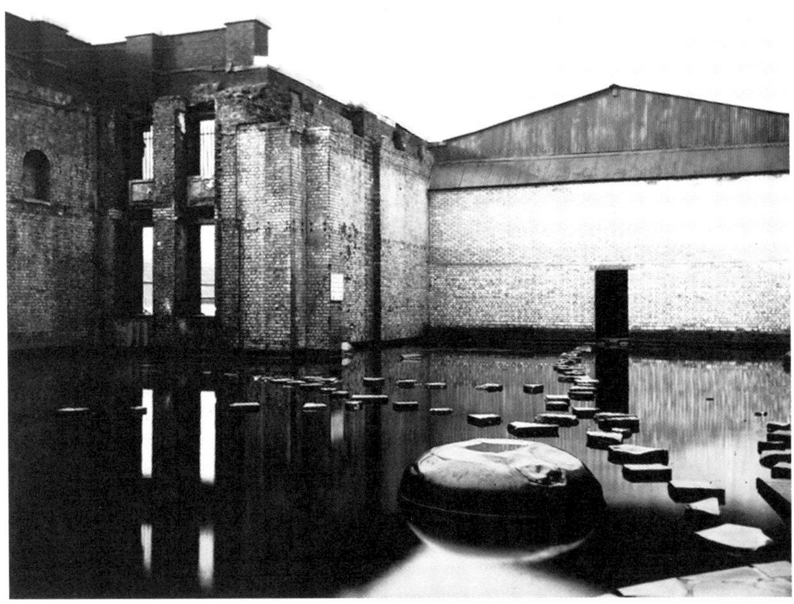

44. *Photographed in 1942, this war-damaged area on the first floor (now the Greek and Roman Life Room and part of the Department of Coins and Medals) remained open to the elements for several years. Sealing the floor had disadvantages: rainfall produced a shallow pond for the warders to navigate. The then Director's children played on the stepping stones.*

incendiaries hit the south-west corner of the building. Around 150,000 books were destroyed, some by fire as the old cast iron bookstack buckled in the intense heat. Other volumes succumbed to water. On the south-west side of the Museum, the roofs of the Coin Room, the upper western range of galleries and the central saloon above the main staircase were lost as incendiaries got into the attic space between the outer copper shell and the ornate plaster ceilings and fires broke out ahead of the Museum's fire-fighters. For years afterwards it was necessary to carry an umbrella when walking through what had been the upper Greek vase rooms. Of the antiquities, however, only a few duplicates were lost, since in the early months of the war the collections had been evacuated to the country or lodged in heavily reinforced basements.

Much of the Museum's energy after the Second World War was taken up with repairing war damage. The four galleries at the top of the main staircase and the upper western range had to be virtually rebuilt in the 1950s and 1960s. Offices for a new Department of Prehistoric and Romano-British Antiquities, practical but entirely lacking in architectural merit (now demolished), were erected just north of the Front Hall extension and opened in 1971.

The decision to reorganize the entire Greek and Roman ground floor display was taken in

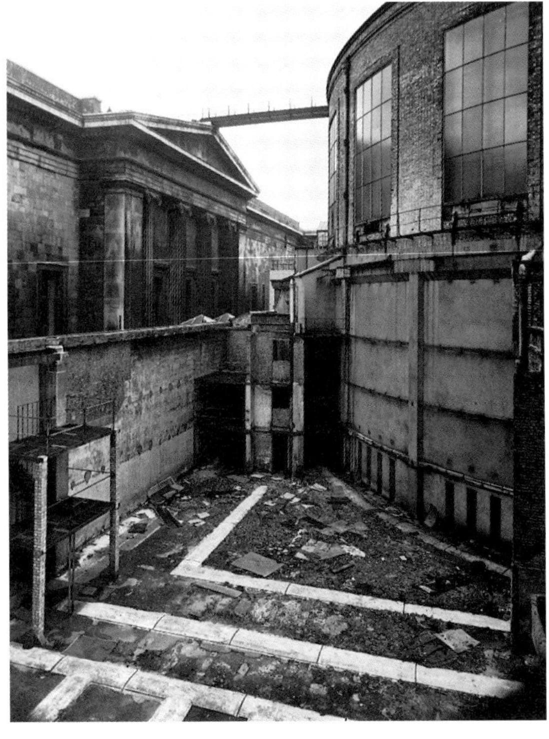

45. *The south-west quadrant, destroyed in 1941, awaits reconstruction in this photograph of 1949 which opened up for the first time since 1855 a view of one of Sir Robert Smirke's inner porticos. The replacement building was subsequently demolished to make way for the Great Court.*

summer 1962. The designers were R. D. Russell and R.Y. Goodden, with associate designer Robin Wade. The new Greek and Roman Galleries were opened by the Duke of Edinburgh on 3 July 1969. The *Sunday Times* (John Russell) remarked:

> Till a week or two ago even boys not yet bearded knew that to say about the B.M. 'Stupendous things, horribly shown'. . . The B.M. was the sleeping beauty among the world's great museums . . . But no longer: the BM has crossed a new frontier with the installation of its Greek and Roman antiquities . . . A poetic idea now rules at the BM.

In 1963 it was also decided that the Assyrian Galleries should be re-floored, re-roofed and re-lit with concealed modern artificial lighting. A new entrance was opened up for the Khorsabad human-headed bulls. Reliefs were replaced according to a carefully thought-out chronological order, described as 'a great reshuffling of the slabs, like cards in a pack'. The work was completed in 1970.

The removal of the ethnographical collections had been under consideration since the nineteenth century. In November 1924 there was a suggestion that one of the principal buildings used during the British Empire Exhibition at Wembley should be converted into an Ethnographical Museum. There were also proposals for a new museum of ethnography at South Kensington, to be built between 1942 and 1946, and the construction of new ethnography galleries on Montague Street. The collections in fact made a thirty-year 'temporary' move to Burlington Gardens (the Museum of Mankind) in 1969/70, thus freeing space for antiquities and special exhibitions in the upper eastern galleries. The Museum of Mankind closed in 1997. The objects will return to Bloomsbury at the end of the century.

The Victorian grime on the façades, familiar to many generations, was removed in 1978, leaving behind a soft grey-white which, when floodlit, glows apricot.

THE BRITISH LIBRARY

When opening the new British Library building at St Pancras on 25 June 1998 Her Majesty The Queen remarked that the engagement had been in the diary 'longer than most'. As we have seen, since the middle of the nineteenth century the idea had been canvassed of rehousing parts of the British Museum on a nearby site. In 1859 consideration was given to securing the site south of the present building, but a Trustees' Committee reluctantly concluded that the estimated cost (£455,000) was too great to be contemplated. The land purchased

46. *Greece and Rome meet Assyria within a 1960s setting.*

47. *The Smirke revival entrance to the Hellenistic Room, the 1960s mezzanine in John Taylor's Mausoleum Room, restored during the early 1990s.*

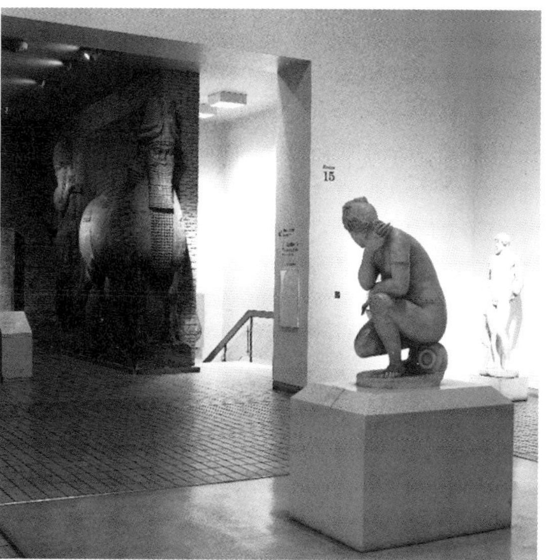

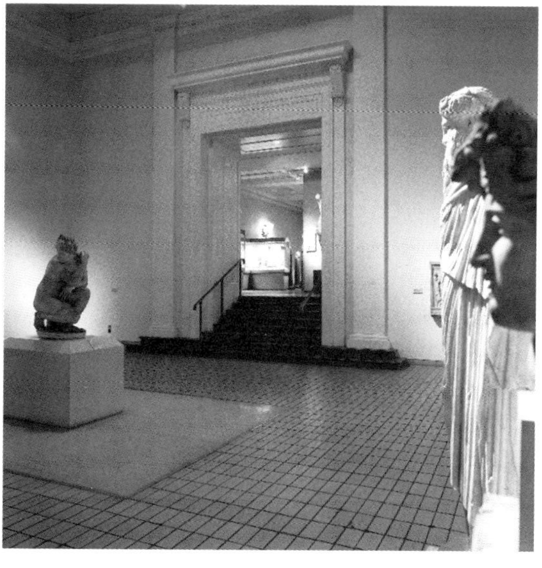

from the Bedford Estates in 1894-5 might have provided a solution, but sufficient funds were not available for its full development and the surrounding houses became subject to preservation orders after the Second World War. In 1943 the Trustees' Sub-Committee on Printed Books, on being informed that even if two quadrant bookstacks were rebuilt this would be sufficient only for thirty years' acqusitions, 'came to the conclusion that the possible removal of the library from the Museum is a question demanding serious consideration'.

Even after the departure of natural history in the 1880s, the continuing dream had been to preserve at least something of the Museum founders' original concept of universality by keeping together the museum and the library, and so strenuous efforts were made to acquire a site in Bloomsbury. On 23 June 1944 the Director, Sir John Forsdyke, wrote to the Ministry of Works proposing a new building to the south of the Museum. The County of London Plan by Sir Patrick Abercrombie and J. H. Forshaw (1944) and Sir Patrick Abercrombie's Greater London Plan (1945) both indicated expansion in the immediate neighbourhood. In the Labour Government's Town and Country Planning Act of 1947 the site south of the Museum was designated in principle. This designation of the site was incorporated in the London County Council's Greater London Development Plan of 1951. The Ministry of Works gradually bought up Bloomsbury freeholds and in August 1962 it appointed two architects – Sir Leslie Martin and Colin St John Wilson – to prepare plans in consultation with a Committee of Trustees. The architects' outline plan was approved by the Trustees on 9 January 1964 and given tentative government approval on 24 September 1964. It consisted of a central pedestrian piazza from the Museum to St George's Church, an underground car-park, a new library on the east side, a new lecture theatre, exhibition building and restaurant on the west, 21 shops or offices and 106 housing units. The new complex was scheduled to be built during the 1970s at an estimated cost of £10 million.

The building was eventually located almost a mile away at St Pancras at a cost of £511 million and opened over thirty years later. The first objections to the plan emerged from the London Borough of Camden in 1965 and from the Minister of Housing, Richard Crossman, in 1966. Plans were drawn and redrawn. A Committee under the chairmanship of Frederick Dainton was set up by the Government in 1967 and reported in 1969, not ruling out the Great Russell Street site. In 1971 a White Paper announcing that the Government had decided to set up a separate organisation to be known as the British Library (incorporating the Museum's library departments and other libraries) was presented to Parliament. This also recommended that the library should be rehoused south of the Museum. The British Library Act was passed in 1972 and the new institution came into being in July 1973 on the assumption that it would be housed in the vicinity of the Museum. However, in 1974 the situation changed. By now the conservation lobby had grown stronger and the Borough of Camden was doggedly determined to oppose the building on the Great Russell Street site. Although about five acres of Bloomsbury had been acquired by the Department of the Environment, there were pockets all over the site which would have to be the subject of compulsory purchase orders, with consequential further public enquiries. Although the British Library Board was still in favour of Bloomsbury, there were pressures on it to look elsewhere, not least the possibility of at last starting work on a new building to absorb expanding collections which had been outhoused all over London. The Museum was consulted and acquiesced in the selection of a site outside Bloomsbury if such were available. On 19 December 1974 the Minister announced that the Government had decided to consider a site for the library at Somers Town on former railway land fronting on to the north side of Euston Road next to St Pancras railway station. In August 1975 the British Library Board accepted this location. The Government's decision to go ahead with a new building there was announced on 7 March 1978.

The new building attracted much criticism as it slowly – very slowly – grew, but its opening silenced most of the detractors.

THE NEW WING

Planning for the so-called New Wing started well over a century before it was erected. In December

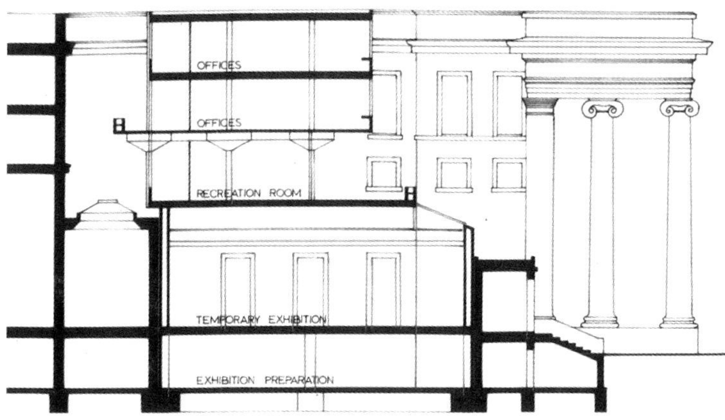

48. *The revised plan for Sir Colin St John Wilson's 'New Wing', juxtaposing 1975 with 1845 and providing desperately needed exhibition and administrative space.*

1851 at a meeting attended by both Sydney Smirke and Richard Westmacott it was recommended that a two-storey building be built to the south of the Lycian Gallery. Despite revived interest in the 1860s, funds were never available and other projects took priority. The original scheme, designed by Colin St John Wilson and prepared in 1969/70, provided for an L-shaped building. Because of limitations on government expenditure in the early 1970s the western arm of the building was deleted, reducing the area to be provided by some 43 per cent. Outline plans for the revised building were completed in November 1973, and funds were made available to construct restaurants, offices, a boardroom and a purpose-built temporary exhibitions gallery. Work began on site in November 1975; the first part of the New Wing to be completed was the Exhibitions Gallery, which was brought into use in November 1978, and the building was formally opened in 1980.

The New Wing cost about £2.5 million to build and equip. It comprises a basement, ground floor and three upper floors, giving a total area of approximately 40,000 square feet (3,716 sq. m). Most of the rooms are new, but it borders on Smirke's western colonnade and has incorporated some old spaces. The old wood-panelled Readers' Admissions desk has gone, as has the richly decorated but acoustically deficient boardroom. The Smirke ceiling has been retained (in some instances rather incongruously, as in one of the lavatories), and the offices of the Department of Greek and Roman Antiquities have been remodelled. The New Wing displaced the basement below what used to be the Graeco-Roman Gallery, which had been used as a public restaurant. Also demolished was the staff canteen, a shed which tended from time to time to attract the notice of the public health authorities.

THE JAPANESE GALLERIES

While being an adaptation rather than an addition, the Japanese Galleries deserve notice as the 'biggest loft conversion in London'. In 1984 a large, empty roof space in King Edward VII's Galleries, left over after the installation of a false ceiling above the Prints and Drawings and Oriental Antiquities Departments, was identified for possible use as a gallery. A feasibility study was commissioned; an appeal for funds was launched and 80 per cent of the money required was raised in Japan. Designs were prepared by Gordon Bowyer & Partners. The start of work was marked in 1987 by a *Kikoshiki* ceremony, to ensure safety during construction, presided over by a Shinto priest from Japan. The gallery was opened on 6 April 1990.

THE HIRAYAMA STUDIO

In 1836 a piece of land was let at a peppercorn rent by the Bedford Estates on the south side of No. 1 Montague Street for the construction of a savings bank. This was duly and elegantly built with a single-storied hall, two pairs of columns supporting the vaulted roof. A waiting room was insisted upon by the Estate to ensure that before the bank opened in the morning customers did not congregate in the street annoying or disturbing the local residents. The building was acquired by the Trustees as part of the 1894-5 purchase from the Estate (p. 57). After a variety of mundane and less mundane uses (it was at one time a drill hall) it was transformed into a studio for the conservation of Eastern pictorial art and opened on 28 September 1994.

THE DRAINS

A review of the building would be incomplete without at least a glimpse of the drains and other services which, while unglamorous, have helped to make the Museum what it is. The sewage and drainage system for Montagu House was, in essence, late seventeenth-century. A series of pipes and cesspits serviced the needs of the building and, with some late eighteenth-century modifications, this system remained until Montagu House was replaced. The situation was made worse by the construction of adjacent houses on the Bedford Estate between the 1770s and early 1800s. In 1810 the architect George Saunders (better known for the Townley Gallery) was much involved with the drains, declaring: 'In my report of March 9 1810, mention is made of the confused state of the old drains & pipes, scarcely in any instance agreeing with the former plan that had been given of them, and of the inconvenience which was occasioned by it . . . The course of every drain and pipe now in use has been carefully traced.' A copy of this plan survives in the archives. It shows a fairly complex system, including drainage pipes in parts of the garden to cope with sections of boggy ground since the water table was high in this area. Smirke reported in 1832 that, 'the average level of the land springs under the site of all the buildings is generally not more than 3 feet (90 cm) below the floor'.

49. *In 1997 archaeologists excavating the east lawn uncovered the conduit which ran under the eastern service wing of Montagu House. This was one of the labyrinth of drains surveyed by an exasperated George Saunders in 1810.*

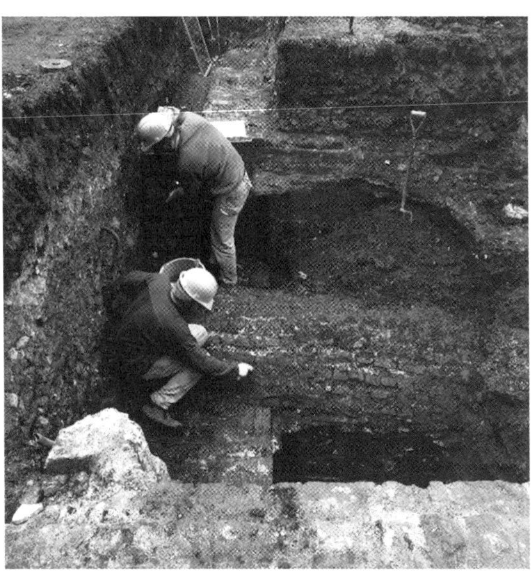

During the 1840s there began a concerted effort to improve the drainage and sewage-disposal facilities in the area: the construction of New Oxford Street (opened in April 1847) resulted in the removal of the insanitary, overpopulated St Giles 'Rookery'. At the Museum there were four on-site wells which provided drinking water. By 1840 a well 'yielding spring-water of very superior quality' existed in an angle at the south-west corner of the old buildings. When Montagu House was taken down, the resinking of this was included in the contract for digging and a pump was provided. In 1906 the pump was replaced and used for several more years. A more general supply was, from 1813, provided by the New River Company. This brought water initially from near Ware in Hertfordshire to a reservoir in Clerkenwell, whence it was distributed by means of wooden conduits and was then fed by pipes into the Museum from a water main running along Great Russell Street. Water was supplied in the staff residences (not in the main house) and a particularly important protection against fire was provided by reservoirs to the east of the building and in the forecourt which supplemented the fire cocks in the courtyard. The New River Company continued to supply water through the mains during the nineteenth century.

The subject of lavatories is a delicate one and has been little explored in previous accounts of the building. There would appear to have been some, but minimal, lavatory facilities available in Montagu House, for in 1811 Saunders reported: 'The water closet proposed to be removed from the great staircase west of the Hall, being for common use, I beg to suggest that it should not be within the house; and that it should not be formed with intricate machinery.' As the water closet was concealed behind the Great Staircase, 'common' probably applied to staff only (who also had facilities in their residences). By the mid-nineteenth century, once the Museum began to open on public holidays, daily attendances estimated at 20,000 or 30,000 were not unusual. The water closet in the garden presumably survived, and there appear to have been some facilities for readers. Edward Hawkins was driven to complain to the Trustees about his residence in 1837: 'Every person calling at his door is liable to witness indecencies and sure to be offended by unpleasant smells, which are frequently perceived even within the House.'

Robert Smirke could not offer a solution, remarking unhelpfully that things should improve when the new Reading Room was constructed. A few lavatories for the entirely male staff were included in Smirke's plans but there seems to have been little else. In May 1842 Edward Gray, Keeper of Zoology, chivalrously offered the water closet in the Bird Room and also that in the passage to the Insect Room for the use of female visitors and students. Robert Smirke thought that any such accommodation would be 'in many respects objectionable', although he offered the hope that something could be done when the entrance to the new building was built. Smirke was, however, sympathetic towards the needs of female students in the Greek and Townley galleries. His offer of the water closet used by the Principal Officer of the Department elicited a response from the curators that 'the proposed appropriation was objectionable on the score of delicacy and that the provision of such convenience might be deferred for the present, if not entirely dispensed with.'

In May 1843 the Trustees asked the Secretary to remind Sir Robert Smirke that, 'it is their wish that ample conveniences ... should be provided for the use of the Establishment of the museum and for all classes of persons who frequent it for the purpose of studying the collections whether literary, scientific or artistical.' By at least 1859 the ladies had a 'cloakroom' off the centre of the upper eastern Zoological Gallery. It was not until 1865, however, that Sydney Smirke submitted plans for public conveniences and hope was expressed of still further extension.

Before the start of the Great Court construction there were well over 100 lavatories scattered throughout the Museum, but very few on the upper levels of the Smirke building, reflecting the initial lack of provision.

HEATING AND VENTILATION

In Montagu House heating and cooking facilities were provided by numerous decorative, but ineffectual, fire-grates and some temperamental open fires and early ranges. Although several 'modern' fire-grates were introduced and a number of fireplaces and flues were sealed up or removed in the 1760s as part of a major fireproofing and underpinning programme, this inadequate and often derided system continued. Open fires remained in the public areas until Montagu House and the Townley Gallery were replaced during the second quarter of the nineteenth century by the Smirke building. At least in some areas, ventilation and heating were very primitive. A reader complained in winter 1819 that in the Reading Room 'frost seized on one of my feet, and had materially affected the other'. In 1820 the 'want of ventilation' and the 'foul state' of the Townley Gallery were referred to the chemist Sir Humphrey Davey who, as President of the Royal Society, was then a Trustee.

In common with much of London, the Museum used child chimney sweeps, but in 1842 the Principal Librarian, Sir Henry Ellis,

> . . . reminded the Trustees that the Act of Parliament [1840] directing the disuse of climbing boys for chimney sweeping would come into operation on 1st July and suggested whether it might not be advisable for Sir Robert Smirke to have such chimneys of the old house as will remain, as well as all the chimneys of the several officers houses examined, and such alterations made as might ensure the effectual sweeping of them in future.

Chimneys in the residential wings and the remaining part of Montagu House were accordingly inspected and altered. Staff studies and residences in the Smirke building remained heated by open fires until relatively recently, with the 'benefits' of patented grates and chimney cowls. There were, however, strict rules about raking them out at night.

Robert Smirke was an innovator in all aspects of building works. This extended to heating, and it is significant that C. J. Richardson's influential work *Warming and Ventilation* (1837) was dedicated to him. Smirke had hot-water central heating installed throughout the new building and various systems were adopted to suit the needs of specific areas. As they all required coals to feed the furnaces and heat the boilers, the Museum's bill from the Gas Light and Coke Company, Westminster, was considerable. Hot water flowed through underfloor pipes covered by iron grilles or, for additional safety, slate. The Trustees took an interest in the design of these grilles, in 1831 directing that Sir Robert Smirke be informed that the grating in the new Elgin Room was 'unsightly . . . and [of] their wish to have a grating of brass . . . more ornamental and less liable to catch the foot of the visitor'. The pipes passed through ingeniously designed pedestal stoves ('chests' of hot water pipes) which were strategically installed in the various galleries (Price and Manby system).

It was not possible to please everyone. On 18 October 1833 Mr Price reported to Sir Robert Smirke on a complaint about the lack of heat in the Print Room:

> On the day that I called the temperature of the room as indicated by the thermometer was 65 degrees, but still Mr Ottley said his feet and hands were cold. As the apparatus was not designed to keep the room at a higher temperature than 60 degrees I cannot I fear, . . . hold out a hope that in the present state, it ever will meet Mr Ottley's wishes.

Smirke had little sympathy, commenting, 'As he [Ottley] appears to require the partial excitement which can be given only by standing or sitting before a fire, no apparatus . . . will relieve him.'

The King's Library and the 1838 Reading Room in the North Wing were heated by hot air, which was introduced via a series of shafts within the walls. As with all these pioneering systems, there were problems. Many complained of the

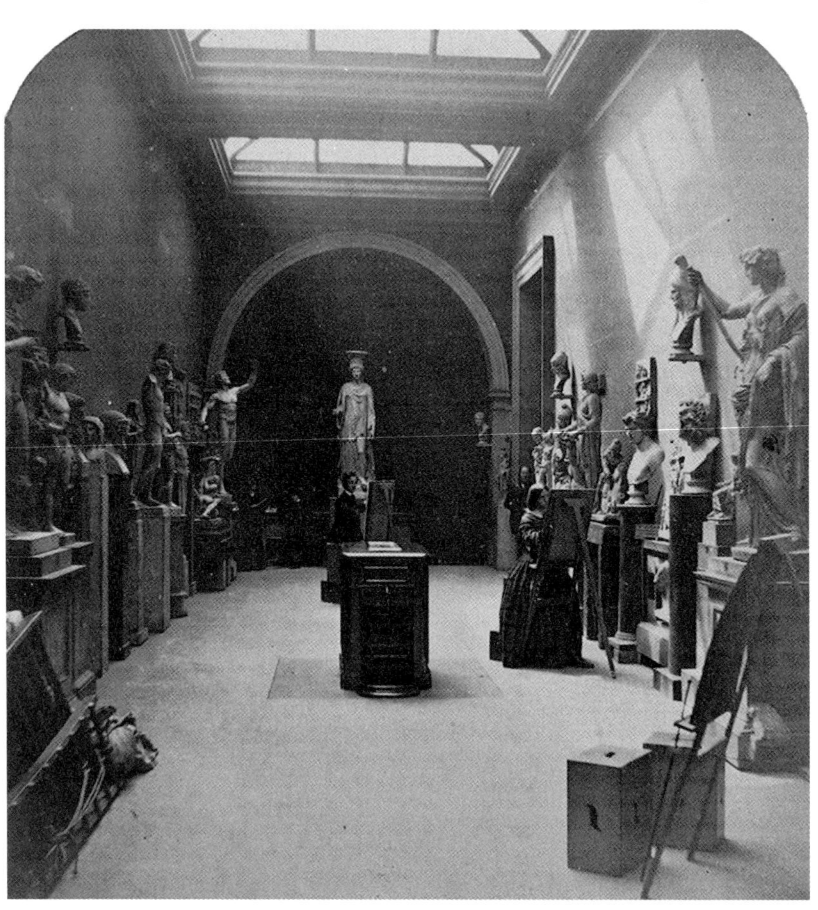

50. *The Third Graeco-Roman Saloon, photographed in 1857 by Roger Fenton, showing artists in the gallery on Students' Day, taking advantage of the natural light falling onto the sculptures. In the centre of the room stands a cast iron stove, a chest of hot-water pipes connected to the underfloor heating system.*

'Museum headache', especially in the flea-infested Reading Room. Its replacement, Sydney Smirke's Round Reading Room (completed 1857), was provided with its own furnaces and an ingenious heating and ventilation system connected to readers' desks. The framework of each table was of iron, forming air-distributing channels controlled by valves, contrived so that the air could be delivered at the top of the screen division above the level of readers' heads. A tubular rail was provided as a footwarmer. There was an outlet on the north side of the North Wing:

> ... the air chamber below [floor level] ... is six feet [1.8 m] high and occupies the whole area of the reading room. It is fitted with hot water pipes arranged in radiating lines. The supply of fresh air is obtained from a shaft 60 ft [18.2 m] high ... about 500 ft [152.4 m] distant, communicating with a tunnel or subway, which has branches or 'loop-lines' fitted with valves for diverting the current.

By 1858 a variety of systems were in use – hot air, hot water in large pipes, hot water at high pressure, open fireplaces with descending flues, and common open fireplaces. The Reading Room system was fed into the King's Library.

But even the Reading Room system was criticized soon after its opening and, in pre-deodorant days, the atmosphere must have been unpleasant. On 27 March 1841 Frederic Madden wrote in his diary: 'The Museum was opened today for the first time in the Easter holidays since it was founded. The day being very fine, although cold, above 24,100 persons visited the Museum between 10 and 4 o'clock. The dust, heat and stench caused by such a crowd was intolerable.' Sydney Smirke reported to the Trustees in 1861 that, 'In the Bird Room the smell from the water closet is getting very offensive and when added to the unavoidable smell of camphor from the objects exhibited, the nuisance is so great this hot weather that I am informed several ladies have fainted.' A letter to the *Builder* in 1870 complained of 'the strong musty smell, at certain times sickening' in the vicinity of the Reading Room and suggested that the Museum should 'fix a few hat pegs in the lavatory. Owing to the absence of these, the scarcity of soap (as a rule) and the dreadfully damp towels, a wash really becomes an unpleasant experience.'

In 1875 the ventilation of the Reading Room was improved through the installation of double-coil hot pipes within the double glazing of the windows. Improvements to the Museum's heating systems continued and costs were significantly reduced through the introduction of Messrs Haden's Hot Water Low-Pressure System to the Assyrian Gallery and the King's Library. This was subsequently extended throughout the building, and the Museum's association with Haden's has continued throughout the twentieth century.

Thankfully, one catastrophe which did not afflict the British Museum was the explosion of a boiler. Elsewhere this was a common occurrence, and in 1865 it was decided that boilers should be inspected regularly at the Museum by the 'Association for the Prevention of Steam Boiler Explosions'. By the 1870s six stokers were employed at the Museum and regular inspections resulted in a reliable service and immediate action when boilers required replacing.

Sir John Burnet, architect of King Edward VII's Galleries (p. 58), was anxious to incorporate modern technology and made a fact-finding visit to several modern museums and galleries in the USA. He was much impressed by what he found, which greatly influenced his choice of services for the new building. It was successfully heated and illuminated to a high standard; a new boiler complex was built to the south of the new galleries and, with necessary upgrading, continues to service the needs of a large part of the Museum.

THE DEPARTURE OF THE BRITISH LIBRARY

The first books left Bloomsbury on 2 December 1996, and on 3 June 1997 the ghost of the failed poet Enoch Soames, Max Beerbohm's 1897 invention who sold his soul to the devil for the opportunity to visit the British Museum Reading Room in a hundred years' time, duly appeared. Soames was only just in time, for on 25 October 1997 the Reading Room closed with a party – a sight not witnessed since it opened to invited guests in May 1857 with champagne served on the catalogue desks. Prior to closing, the room began to fill up as many decades of readers and staff gathered for the final bell. When all books had been returned, book trollies of sparkling wine emerged from the Sorting Passage and in the end it proved rather

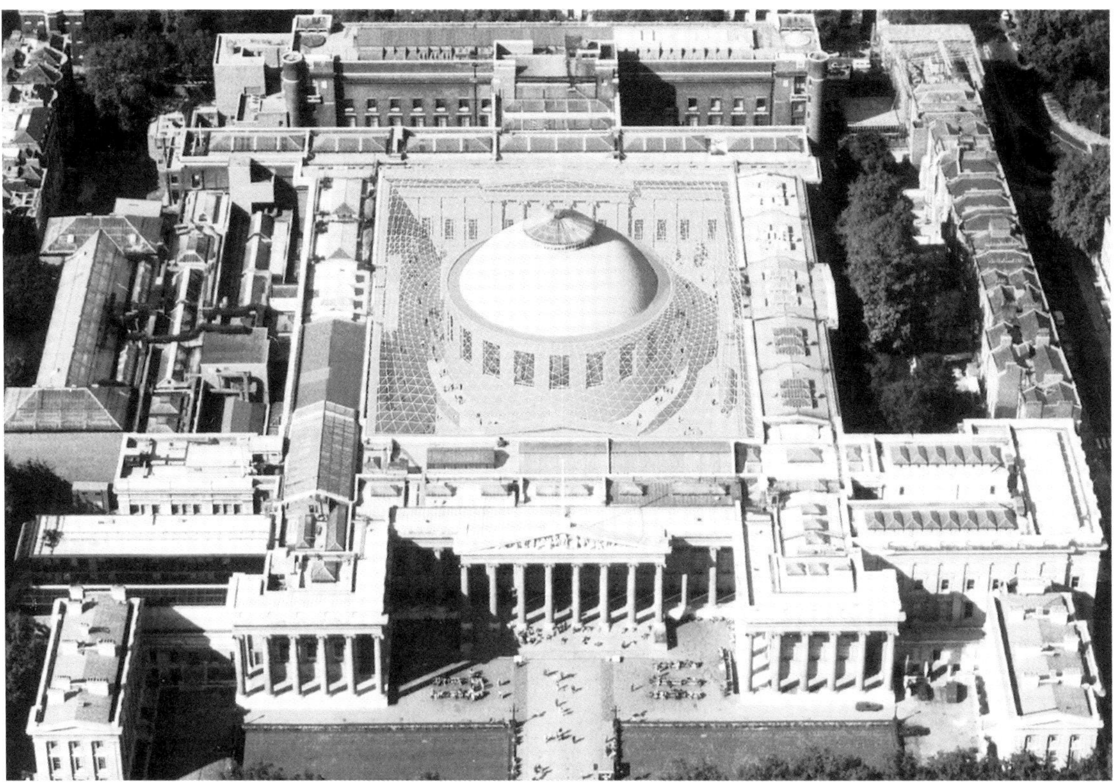

difficult to remove the very last readers. The following day a performance of Handel's *Messiah* provided a more solemn close.

51. *A computer-simulated impression of the completed Great Court.*

THE GREAT COURT AND BEYOND

The 250th Anniversary programme of development, of which the Great Court project is the centrepiece, is the largest building project in the Museum since the nineteenth century. The statistics are equally impressive:

- The inner courtyard of the Museum is 100 metres long and 70 metres wide, the size of Wembley football pitch or Hanover Square.
- 16,000 tonnes of concrete will be used to build the foundations and new ground floor inside the courtyard.
- The glass roof, weighing around 1,000 tonnes, will be supported on 10 kilometres of steel and covers an area of 6,000 square metres.
- The roof will contain 12,000 square metres of glass, enough to glaze about 500 domestic greenhouses; the glass will be composed of around 3,500 individual pieces of glass, each one a unique triangle.

The project is supported by funds from the Millennium Commission and the Heritage Lottery Fund. Support has also come from a pre-eminent private donor and a number of generous benefactors, all of whose names will be recorded on the building.

The proposal to roof over Smirke's courtyard is not in fact new, the earliest schemes having emerged in the 1830s. In 1850 'Quondam' wrote to the *Builder* suggesting that:

> The great internal courtyard if covered with a glass dome would give room for the whole contents of the national collection; an ample causeway might be reserved all round . . . With four entrances from the centres of the square it would be accessible on all sides, and being covered in with pellucid glass

> this colossal hall whatever its height, could obstruct no light from the windows of the present structure. Ornamentation to any extent might be introduced in stained glass.

In 1854 Sir Charles Barry (1795-1860), having been asked by the Office of Woods and Forests to comment on Sydney Smirke's and Antonio Panizzi's proposals for the Round Reading Room (p. 46), himself put forward a scheme for covering the inner quadrangle with a glass roof to provide a hall 'covered wholly with glass and laid out ornamentally with fine sculpture'. This was treated with some disdain by Sydney Smirke, who was determined that the Round Reading Room should go ahead. While greeting it, somewhat sarcastically, as a 'captivating idea', Smirke expressed concern about ventilation, heating and (in pre-electric times) lighting.

Smirke and Panizzi won the argument, but even with the Reading Room and bookstacks in place there was still an unused area around them. In 1857, with the Trustees even more desperate for space, a tentative proposal was put forward to glaze the area surrounding the dome. Sydney Smirke was asked to prepare estimates for the west side, but this proposal did not go very far and later in the year the Trustees were again reminded 'that there would be great difficulty in ventilating the space so glazed over, in providing against the diminution of light to the surrounding basement of the main building and in remedying the inconvenience that might arise for want of free external access to the new building.'

The proposal had long been forgotten when in the late 1980s the Trustees began to plan for the use of the space vacated by the British Library. The initial concept was to construct new floors within the bookstack space. However, with the advantages of modern technology, a more imaginative approach could be suggested of looking beyond the shabby buildings surrounding the dome and taking advantage of the courtyard's vast space. In 1993 an international competition was announced for the appointment of a consultant architect to consider how best the 'Great Court' (a name with echoes of Montagu House) should function when it became available. In July 1994 the winner, Norman Foster and Partners, was announced. Their solution was to roof over the Court, to open the area around the Round Reading Room to the public, to build a semi-ellipse of facilities around the Reading Room drum (including the Sir Joseph Hotung Exhibition Gallery), and to provide educational and gallery facilities below ground level (see p. 46). Work began on site on 2 March 1998, and the first concrete for the new building was poured on 7 August.

The Study Centre

In September 1995 the Museum purchased the 1960s former Royal Mail West Central Sorting Office on New Oxford Street. This will bring together, in 21,000 square metres of new facilities, study collections housed at four different London locations and, it is hoped, include adequate space for future acquisitions. The project will be carried out under the 'Private Finance Initiative' and with grants from the Heritage Lottery Fund and the Clothworkers' Foundation.

DIGGING UP THE BRITISH MUSEUM

To fulfil the legal requirements of the Great Court project a programme of on-site archaeological investigation and rescue work has been undertaken. Paradoxically, although the Museum has excavated all over the world it had never systematically looked at its own site. Basements, lawns and inner roads have been beset with deep trenches full of archaeologists. Remnant walls of Montagu House have been found south of the present building: the finds provide a valuable record of the various stages of the Museum. Portland stone, marble, brick and ornamental plasterwork in the forecourt; bases of cast iron columns in the north-west basement – all these offer a tantalising glimpse of the long-gone British Museum. The lack of any quantity of objects confirms that the various sales of building materials held in the past were a success for the Museum and the Treasury.

It is evident from archaeological work and from searching through the various reports of a succession of architects and surveyors that the extent of the building work at the Museum during the last two centuries has resulted in an alteration in the ground level and, to a certain extent, the surface layer of the site. Both Robert and Sydney Smirke had to bring in (and recycle) ballast and earth to alter ground levels and construct deep foundations,

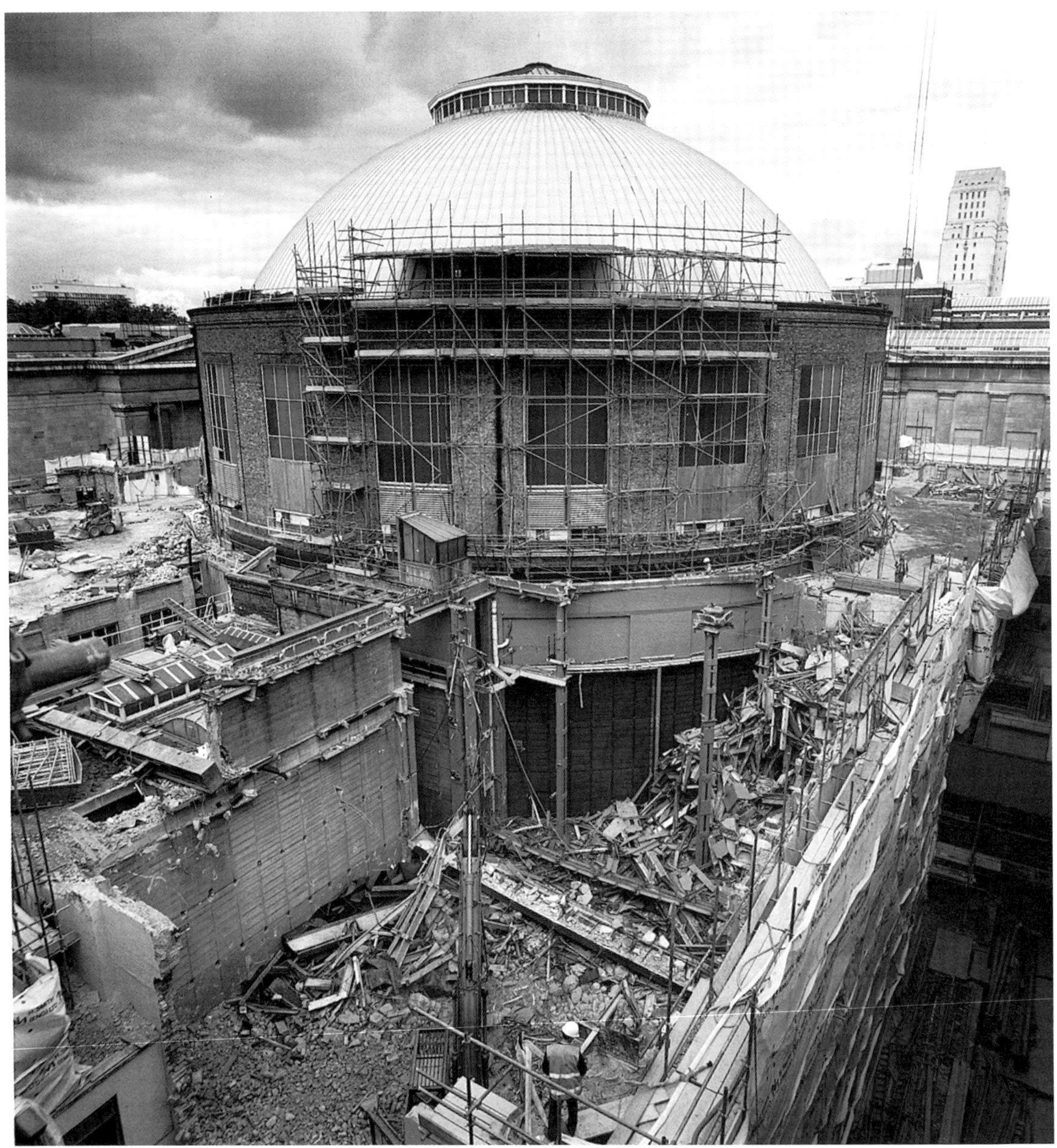

52. *The demolition of the south-east bookstack and the offices of the Department of Prehistoric and Romano-British Antiquities, 1998.*

in some instances to a depth of 12 feet (3.6 m). Similarly, Sydney was directed to acquire a quantity of topsoil to dress the proposed grass plots (once the Trustees had decided on lawns for the forecourt) and, annoyingly, soon after remove good topsoil from the inner quadrangle during the construction of the Round Reading Room. However, Sir John Burnet had the most frustrating of tasks: the ground floor of his extension facing Montague Place was lower than the buildings that it replaced. Complex negotiations with London County Council and Holborn Borough Council eventually resulted in an agreement to lower the road level. Living in one of the two remaining houses in Montague Place (to the west of his building under construction), Burnet in February 1909 witnessed to his horror workmen from Holborn Borough Council arriving and proceeding to re-lay the road to the original level. During the following month his pleas to the Director, the Trustees, the LCC and Holborn and a 'conference' of all concerned proved successful and an 'alteration . . . of material importance', namely the lowering of the road by 8½ inches (21.5 cm), was satisfactorily undertaken.

ENVOI

This has been of necessity a brief summary of the building's history. While Robert Smirke's basic design remains, very many alterations have been made. One has only to stand outside and see the bricked-up windows, the different shades of brickwork, and inside, ceilings replaced because of wartime damage, mezzanines which have added much-needed space, doors which do not appear on the early plans and hidden windows which do. It is, however, still the largest neo-classical building in the British Isles and it still possesses the same 'dignified grandeur' it had when first built.

53. *Before the rebuilding of the south portico, plaster casts were made of details from the three surviving porticos. Here casts are carefully compared with the originals before ovolo fillet and bead, ogees and beaded astragals are painstakingly carved off-site by stonemasons.*

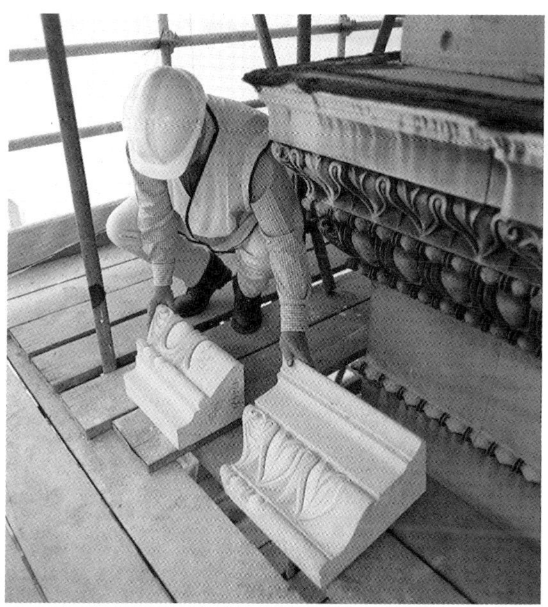

What would the ghosts of the past recognize? Those from the eighteenth century, thanks to excavations for the Great Court, might have a glimpse of the familiar red brick of Montagu House emerging (along with clay pipes and oyster shells) after almost a century and a half underground. They might also recognize some storage presses in the Print Room which, in spite of many moves, still survive – but nothing else remains.

The King's Library is much as it was, even though the original books have gone. Indeed, the removal of British Library exhibition cases enables the visitor to appreciate its great size and the grandeur it possessed prior to nineteenth- and twentieth-century encroachments. Most of Smirke's galleries survive, although they have been redesigned and repainted. There are a few original Smirke display cases exhibiting vases and other artefacts in the upper gallery devoted to the Greeks in Southern Italy, and the ceilings of Smirke's upper eastern and western galleries are being restored. Antonio Panizzi would recognize the former office of the Keeper of Printed Books, first occupied by him almost 150 years ago, in the low galleries adjacent to the King's Library. Burnet's Print Gallery has gone, but the adjacent Print Room would not be unfamiliar to him and the Joseph E. Hotung Gallery of Oriental Antiquities has revived his splendid Edwardian style. The railings and the still empty plinths continue to front Great Russell Street, although some sections are pitted by bomb damage which occurred during the Second World War. A flagpole, rather than Britannia, surmounts the pediment, and the frieze along the colonnade remains undressed. Smirke's colonnade itself remains, although its cleaned appearance would surprise those who saw it covered in black velvet soot after its first decade of Victorian pollution.

In some instances the past is to be restored. In the quadrangle Smirke's southern portico will be rebuilt and the twentieth-century windows on the northern wall will disappear. Above all, the Great Court in the centre of the Museum will open to visitors, as Smirke intended.

FURTHER READING

Marjorie Caygill, *The Story of the British Museum*, 2nd edn, British Museum Press, London, 1992.

J. Mordaunt Crook, *The British Museum: a case-study in architectural politics*, Penguin, Harmondsworth, 1972.

Robert Cowtan, *Memories of the British Museum*, Bentley, London, 1872.

Edward Edwards, *Lives of the Founders, and Notes of some Chief Benefactors and Organizers of the British Museum*, Trubner & Co., London, 1870 (repr. 1969).

P. R. Harris, *The Reading Room*, British Library, London, 1986.

P. R. Harris, *A History of the British Museum Library 1753-1973*, British Library, London, 1998.

Ian Jenkins, *Archaeologists and Aesthetes: in the Sculpture Galleries of the British Museum 1800-1939*, British Museum Press, London, 1992.

Edward Miller, *That Noble Cabinet: a history of the British Museum*, Deutsch, London, 1973.

Elaine M. Paintin, *The King's Library*, British Library, London, 1989.

Unpublished sources include

AOC Archaeology Limited (Charles Le Quesne and John Maloney), 'British Museum Millennium Project – The Great Court and Main Forecourt: An Archaeological Assessment', January 1995 (limited circulation).

British Museum Central Archive.

Diaries of Sir Frederic Madden, Bodleian Library, Oxford, MSS Eng. Hist. C. 140-182.

Sir Edward Maunde Thompson, 'History of the British Museum' (unfinished manuscript), British Library, Department of Manuscripts, Add. MS 52292.

ILLUSTRATION ACKNOWLEDGMENTS

All illustrations are from the British Museum collections except figs 2 (whereabouts unknown) and 5 (Scottish National Photography Collection, Scottish National Portrait Gallery).

INDEX